THIS BOOK BELONGS TO:

Barbara Rice

©IF13103

J U L I A
MORGAN

JULIA MORGAN

Architect of Dreams

GINGER WADSWORTH

LERNER PUBLICATIONS COMPANY • MINNEAPOLIS

In memory of
Hal G. Evarts, Jr.
writer... father... friend

The author would like to extend special thanks to the following people:
Sara Boutelle; Nancy Loe and staff at the Special Collections and
University Archives, Robert Kennedy Library at California Polytechnic
State University; the Bancroft Library's Regional Oral History Project at
the University of California, Berkeley; Robert Pavlik, State Historian at
San Simeon, California; Mary Grace Barron, real estate agent in Calistoga,
California; and my many friends who have helped during this project.

LIBRARY OF CONGRESS CATALOGING-IN-PUBLICATION DATA

Wadsworth, Ginger.
  Julia Morgan, architect of dreams / Ginger Wadsworth.
    p.   cm.
  Includes bibliographical references (p.
  Summary: Recounts the life of the architect whose projects
included designing the Hearst Castle at San Simeon, California.
  ISBN 0-8225-4903-4
  1. Morgan, Julia, 1872-1957—Juvenile literature. 2. Architects—
California—Biography—Juvenile literature. [1. Morgan, Julia,
1872-1957. 2. Architects.] I. Title.
NA737.M68W33   1990
720.92—dc20
[B]
[92]   89-13732
                                                              CIP
                                                               AC
Manufactured in the United States of America

2 3 4 5 6 7 8 9 10 99 98 97 96 95 94 93 92 91

Contents

In the summer of 1878, Julia's mother took her children to New York to live with her parents, the Parmelees, for a year. This studio photograph of six-year-old Julia was taken there.

ONE

A Privileged Child

1872-1890

The elderly lady gathered her staff around her. At first glance she resembled an old-fashioned school teacher, with her wire-rim glasses and her gray hair worn in a bun at the back of her neck. She wore a blue, tailored suit and a white silk blouse. Her pockets bulged with pens, pencils, and sketch pads because she refused to carry a purse.

Julia Morgan cleared her throat and announced that she was retiring as an architect and closing her San Francisco office. She told them that if any clients wanted their drawings or blueprints back, to let her know. Otherwise she would destroy them.

During her career of 47 years, this woman who "looked like a nobody" designed more than 700 buildings—at a time when few women were architects. She shunned publicity and sought anonymity. She avoided the press and refused to have her name posted at construction sites.

Miss Morgan, as she was called by clients and employees, earned a reputation as a "client's architect." She built for her clients, allowing them to determine what the building would look like. No job was too small or too difficult. Julia Morgan's talents ranged from designing a playhouse for her taxi driver's daughters to directing the construction of a California castle for one of the wealthiest men in America.

Before she left the room that day in 1951, she said as she had throughout her career, "My buildings will be my legacy... they will speak for me long after I'm gone."

In 1867, Julia's father, Charles Morgan, sailed from Connecticut around the tip of South America to California. A short, dapper, mining engineer from New England, Charles was convinced that he could make a fortune in minerals. He was not alone. Since 1848, when gold had been discovered in California, thousands of people had flocked to the West Coast.

Although the peak of California's gold rush was over when Charles Morgan arrived, new veins of gold and silver were being discovered throughout the West. Mining corporations were popping up everywhere and experts were being hired to run the mines. Charles was challenged by everything he saw and knew he could find work easily. It would be a perfect place to raise a family.

Charles Morgan returned home and married Eliza Parmelee. He raved about San Francisco—the beautiful city overlooking the Pacific Ocean. He told Eliza about the mansions built by people who had "struck it rich" in the mines. Gold was changing the West, he said, and he wanted to be part of it. They made plans to move to San Francisco.

Eliza's parents were not particularly happy about the marriage but they knew their daughter had a mind of her own. San Francisco was far away and, despite Charles's description, they felt that it was still a rough place, full of miners and other fortune-seekers.

Albert Parmelee, Eliza's father, was a self-made millionaire. He had earned his fortune buying and selling cotton in the South before the Civil War. He loved to pamper his family, especially Eliza. And he did not want that to change.

Before the honeymooners left, Albert Parmelee took his daughter aside and handed her an envelope of money. He told his daughter to buy whatever she needed, and he promised to send more later.

In 1870, Charles and Eliza Morgan moved into a posh, family-oriented hotel on Market Street in downtown San Francisco. While Charles bought and sold mining stock, often unsuccessfully, Eliza purchased furniture and clothes and hired servants.

Parmelee was born in 1870. Two years later, on January 20, 1872, Julia was born. It was time for the Morgans to move.

They built a house across the San Francisco Bay in the fashionable suburb of Oakland. It was a large, three-story house in the latest Victorian style, Eastlake Stick, with ornate wooden trim inside and out.

Eliza rose early to get her children ready for their day and her husband off to work. Charles rode the ferry across the bay to his San Francisco office, where he tried a variety of money-making schemes. For a while, he "thought he was going to be a sugar broker and he had ideas that he might be headquartered in the [Hawaiian] Islands. But that didn't materialize and he didn't make it as a sugar broker." He earned the reputation that if it was something that wasn't going to work, then Charles was in on it. Even so, everyone said that Charles Morgan "was a good-natured man with a lot of friends, and if his failures got to him, he didn't show it."

A tiny woman, Eliza Morgan ruled the household with an iron will. She made sure that the servants kept up with the laundry, cleaning, cooking, and that they maintained the horses and carriage house. Eliza also controlled the household spending with money from her father.

Each time a Morgan child was born, the Parmelees sent money to their daughter so her family could travel East on the new transcontinental railroad, which had been finished in 1869. The Parmelees insisted that their grandchildren be christened in the family church in New York, not in California.

In the summer of 1878, Eliza Morgan and the children moved to the East for a year, being supported and pampered by Julia's grandfather. Charles Morgan had invested unwisely again, this time by buying an unproductive gold mine. Eliza and the children stayed in Morristown, New Jersey, for the

From left to right, *Parmelee, Emma, and Julia pose for a photograph at Emma's christening in New York.*

summer, then traveled back to New York by private railway car, ferry, and carriage. They shopped at the best New York stores and Parmelee went to a private school nearby.

That winter in New York, Julia came down with scarlet fever and was bedridden for several weeks. She had frequent ear infections. One of her cousins died of diphtheria. Clothes and bedding were continually boiled in carbolic acid to stop the spread of disease. Her mother burned her hands severely in a fire, so several servants, including a nurse, waited on Mrs. Morgan and Julia.

Tired of being sick and cooped up inside, Julia missed her father's happy-go-lucky spirit. Mrs. Morgan wrote her husband in January, "Dear Boy... [Julia] denies herself stories, fearing there'll be no more left for Papa to read.... Your Girl, Eliza."

In the summer of 1879, Eliza Morgan returned to the West Coast with her children. Over the years, the Morgans made many cross-country trips to New York. On several occasions, Julia visited her cousin, Lucy Thornton, who had married Pierre LeBrun, a member of a distinguished architectural firm in New York. Julia liked her older cousins from the first time she met them, and would correspond with Lucy and Pierre for many years.

Even though she had servants to take care of their house in Oakland, Eliza Morgan gave all her children jobs to teach them responsibility. Once a week, Julia polished and waxed the banisters, the hand railings that ran next to each flight of stairs.

One Saturday, she heard Parmelee calling her nickname, "Dudu." Julia ran to a window. Three stories below, Parmelee stood on the lawn. He leaned on a rake. Next to him was their younger brother, Avery.

Pushing the window open, Julia saw a carriage on the wide tree-lined street. She waited for the clippety-clop sound of the horses' hooves to fade away. She yelled to her brothers to wait for her, saying that she would have to dust the railings first, then she would come out.

Red, gold, and yellow leaves covered the ground. The boys were supposed to be raking them into great piles. Julia spotted her little sister, Emma, running through the leaves. It was not fair, she thought to herself. Everyone had an outside job except her. She had not been sick for a long time.

Julia returned to her job of dusting the ornate knobs and designs on the handrail. She polished the third floor railing, then started on the second story. Still grumbling, Julia told herself that if she grew up to be an architect and design houses like her cousin Pierre, she would not build any fancy railings for little girls to dust.

That autumn day in 1880, after she finished the dusting, Julia slipped on her coat and muffler, in case she ran into her mother on the way out. That way, her mother could not fuss over her, she thought, and worry about her getting sick.

Julia tiptoed down the hall. She overheard her mother and another lady talking. If she had to play the piano for her Mama. . . .

Julia opened the door slowly. Outside, she lifted her skirt and petticoats and raced into the barn, followed by Parmelee and Avery. She dropped her coat and headed toward the gymnasium equipment her father had set up for her brothers. She would try the balance beam first, she told them, then the rope swing. The boys did not argue with their athletic sister. Even though she was tiny, with pale skin and fine blond hair, her voice rang with authority. As usual, Julia got her way.

Julia Morgan at age seven

In grammar school, Julia continued to be a tomboy. She ignored her sister, Emma. She was as stubborn as she was fearless, and she preferred to run around with her brothers.

The Morgan children went to Oakland's public grammar school and high school. Because all the families in Julia's neighborhood were wealthy, the public schools were considered as exclusive as private schools.

At the time, only the children from upper-class families could attend school regularly. Less wealthy children helped out at home or worked in factories when money was tight. They went to school when they could.

Eventually, Julia outgrew her tomboy ways. She loved school and poured all her energy into her studies. And her parents encouraged her. Eliza and Charles Morgan strongly believed in education for all their children, at a time when girls in particular were not encouraged to graduate from high school.

For most of her life, Julia lived with her family in this house on 14th and Brush streets in Oakland.

By the time she reached Oakland High School, Julia was learning advanced math, physics, Latin, and German. Unlike many of her girlfriends, who were interested in parties, clothes, and watching young men, Julia loved to study. In fact, when it came to homework, she was a perfectionist. After school, she took dancing, violin, and piano lessons, as did her siblings and friends.

Emma, too, awed her classmates with her scholastic abilities. People commented that the Morgan girls were smart, especially Julia. At the same time, they quietly noted that Parmelee, Avery, and Sam, the youngest member of the family, were average students. Like their father, the boys were more easy-going and did not have the drive to succeed.

Eliza Morgan encouraged her brilliant daughters to achieve, and the three Morgan women developed a close-knit relationship.

When Julia was in her last year at Oakland High School, she and her mother discussed Julia's future. Back then, it was traditional for 18-year-old girls to be debutantes and to have "coming out" parties. Their parents were formally presenting them to society and saying that their daughters were ready to meet young men and think about marriage.

As in her tomboy days, Julia rebelled. She told her mother she loved school—she enjoyed studying, especially complicated math problems. And she was a good student. Times were changing. More and more women were going to college, so why couldn't she?

Eliza Morgan did not know what to say at first. Most mothers at that time wanted their daughters to travel and attend parties while looking for a suitable husband.

Julia argued that, unlike many of her friends, she did not enjoy parties. In fact, she felt awkward and shy in large groups. She wanted a career first...maybe in music or medicine... but she was not sure yet.

She reminded her mother about the University of California. Located near Oakland in the city of Berkeley, the campus had opened in 1868. Although most of the students were men, about 100 women were enrolled there.

Mrs. Morgan recognized and admired her daughter's determination to attend college and have a career. She felt it did not matter what Julia decided to do. She had fantastic willpower. Anything would be possible.

In 1890, Julia graduated from Oakland High and told everyone that, like her brother Parmelee and some of her classmates, she was going to the University of California.

Julia stands in front of Notre Dame in Paris, right. *She drew buildings of all kinds, such as this watercolor,* below, *during her studies in Paris.*

TWO

From Berkeley to Paris

1890-1902

For the last time, Julia glanced at herself in the mirror. Yes, her sailor hat was on straight and her suit was spotless. She hurried out to the front porch where Avery waited. A warm September breeze stirred up dust on the streets.

Julia and Avery climbed into a horse-drawn streetcar in front of their house. As they turned the corner, and her house disappeared from view, Julia's stomach knotted. A different kind of life was ahead of her, one she wanted. Yet she was both nervous and excited. Julia was glad that her parents had insisted that Avery escort her to and from college.

Julia hoped to spot one familiar face. Her childhood friend, Jessica Peixotto, was majoring in economics at the University of California. They were sure to share some classes.

As the streetcar drew closer to the campus, Julia looked at the half-dozen stone buildings on the barren hillside. There! That was where she would be studying math—over there was the science building. She could hardly wait.

For Julia, from the first day, her time in school sped by quickly. She liked her classes and her teachers. In the lecture halls, she would lean forward in her desk to hear every word. She took detailed notes. Every evening, she retreated to her bedroom to do her homework and review what she had learned.

Julia took classes in math and science because they were her favorite subjects. At that time, they were unusual fields for a woman to study. As a result, Julia was often the only woman in the room. Many men resented her. Some made rude comments and glared when she took her seat in the classroom. Hard as it was, she learned to ignore them.

Slowly, Julia began to meet some of the students. Many of the women were like herself, from wealthy and socially prominent families. Others came from low-income families.

Julia Morgan, standing, left, *and her Kappa Alpha Theta sorority sisters in 1894*

For the first time, Julia understood how lucky she was to have her parents' money and social status behind her, and even to have the chance to go to school.

At the beginning of her second year, Julia joined the Kappa Alpha Theta sorority and her parents no longer demanded that Avery escort her around the campus. The 27 women in the sorority, or social organization for female students, rented their own house on the edge of the campus and hired a cook-housekeeper. Julia formed a lifelong bond with many of her sorority sisters.

That year, Julia probably met Phoebe Hearst, a wealthy widow who supported numerous charities. She had a home next to the campus and opened it to students. The young women gathered at "Mrs. Hearst's" to talk, for tea parties and musicales, and for a chance to see her fabulous art collection.

Still shy with people outside her immediate family, Julia spent much of her time studying. As one friend recalled, "If she went to parties, she didn't enjoy them...at all." Once in a while, she went on dates, arranged through her sorority.

As an undergraduate student, Julia told her parents she wanted to become an architect. Her mother asked if it were because of Pierre LeBrun.

Julia acknowledged that it was, in part. She had enjoyed the New York visits, where she had been impressed by the architecture he had done. She also liked knowing how things worked and wanted to study electricity, heat, magnetism, mechanics, and sound—branches of physics.

Julia tried to explain that designing a building from the ground up was exciting and challenging, similar to figuring out a complicated math problem. In her mind, she could work out everything step by step, like a composer writing a symphony. With a building, she told her parents, you have a finished product—something you can see—and use for a long time.

Her parents just shook their heads. Yes, Julia was different—different from her brothers and sister—and different from her friends. Unconventional as their daughter was, the Morgans loved her and supported her financially.

Since the university had no architecture school, Julia enrolled in the closest thing, the College of Engineering. In her engineering classes she listened to professors lecture about building materials and structural stress.

When Julia was a senior, she met 32-year-old Bernard Maybeck, an architect hired by the school to teach geometry. Maybeck was a bearded, free-spirited man who dressed in a Chinese jacket and a Scottish cap with a pompon in the center.

Julia was fascinated by Bernard Maybeck as a person and as an architect. With other engineering students, she attended informal architectural classes in his home. She loved the way he designed his unique redwood houses to look as if they were climbing the hills of Berkeley. His philosophy, which Julia adopted, was that houses should look as if they grew on the land.

In the spring of 1894, Julia received her diploma from the University of California. She was the only woman to graduate from the College of Engineering that year.

Maybeck, the son of a German woodcarver, had plans for his favorite pupil. He told Julia that she was very talented. Maybeck encouraged her to continue her education by going to Paris and studying architecture at the Ecole des Beaux-Arts as he had done. It was the finest architectural school in the world. As always, Julia talked it over with her mother. Eliza Morgan agreed with Maybeck. She suggested that Julia go to the East Coast and look at colleges that had architectural programs, then go to Paris. Both Eliza and Charles recognized Julia's talent and determination, just as her teachers had.

In March 1896, Julia and her friend Jessica Peixotto said goodbye to their families and climbed aboard the transcontinental train. Jessica intended to do graduate work in economics in France. As the train sped east, Julia wrote she was "never going write anything about homesickness." For several years, she kept that vow.

After touring colleges, Julia visited her cousins, Lucy and Pierre LeBrun. Pierre encouraged his young cousin in her career choice. They promised to write each other.

When Julia and Jessica sailed for France, the society page of an Oakland paper reported:

> Miss Julia Morgan['s]... destination is Paris, where she will spend a year in close study... Oakland will expect and receive much in the future along architectural lines from so thorough and good a student.

An identification-card photograph of Julia Morgan, taken during her time in Paris

At the Ecole des Beaux-Arts, Julia presented her qualifications, including letters from her instructors and supporters. To her dismay, she discovered that the 250-year-old fine arts school discouraged foreign students. And the school was certainly not ready to accept a woman into its all-male ranks.

Since Beaux-Arts did not have a specific rule barring women, Julia told the school officials she intended to take the entrance exam. After all, she had traveled all the way from California to study architecture.

While angry officials stalled with their answer, Julia began to study French in preparation for the exam. Weeks lengthened into months. The money Julia had brought for a year of study was melting away, so she moved into a small apartment in the student section on the Left Bank of the Seine River. It was a startling contrast to her wealthy, pampered childhood.

Julia refused to ask her family for money even though they easily could have helped her. She did not think it was fair to her brothers and sister. At that time, Avery and Emma were studying at the University of California.

To prepare for the entrance examinations, she worked in an *atelier*, or studio, of an architect. The head of the atelier invited Beaux-Arts students to pay for the instruction and the experience they would gain by working for him. Julia was the only woman in the atelier.

She soon learned that the atelier was a very rough place. The young men liked to play pranks to relieve the tension of the long working hours. They would dump buckets of water on each other or push each other off their long work benches. As the only female, Julia was excluded from their games.

Often homesick and lonely, Julia fought off these feelings and resisted writing about them in her frequent letters

Julia painted this watercolor for an assignment at the Ecole des Beaux-Arts.

home. Instead, she relied on family news from her mother and others back in the United States to keep her in touch with their lives.

In between work and studies, Julia explored Paris and Europe, always carrying a sketch pad and pencil with which to capture a building or part of a building that interested her. She carefully accounted for every penny she spent on her travels and daily living, and often went without a meal in order to buy architectural books.

Julia wrote Lucy and Pierre LeBrun, saying, "I'm so glad I came. It wakes one up so wonderfully." Everything about Europe, Paris, and even the Ecole des Beaux-Arts, was so much more exciting than what she had seen in the United States.

The school finally decided to let women take the entrance exams in the autumn of 1897. During the test, Julia struggled with the math, which was calculated in metrics. As a result, she placed 42nd out of 376 students. That was not good enough. The Ecole took only the top 30.

She tried again in April 1898 and failed. On her third try in October, she was ranked 13th.

The *San Francisco Examiner* headline read:

> CALIFORNIA GIRL WINS HIGH HONOR
> Another California girl is added to the long list of those who have won honor for themselves and for their State abroad. The latest on the list is Miss Julia Morgan, who has just successfully passed the entrance examinations for the Ecole des Beaux-Arts, department of Architecture.... Miss Morgan is the first woman in the world to be admitted to this special department.

A letter to Lucy and Pierre revealed the real story.

> The oral examination ... is the most trying ordeal for its simpleness. There were thirteen examined before me ... and everyone failed entirely — those big strong fellows would get up, tremble, turn white, clutch their hands and seem to have no thinking power left.... When I was called ... I discovered that my hand was rattling in the air, and the discovery so surprised me, I could not do any more mathematics — it was enough for a pretty good mark, but you see so many [students] did nothing.

Now, Julia had a new challenge ahead. The Ecole did not allow students older than 30 to enter competitions and accumulate points toward a certificate of graduation. Racing against time, she had less than three years to complete her studies.

In the midst of Julia's studies, the Maybecks and Phoebe Hearst came to Paris in 1899. Hearst was sponsoring an international architectural competition for a new building program at the Berkeley campus of the University of California.

Phoebe Hearst took an immediate and lasting interest in Julia's ambitious goals. Before leaving Paris, she offered Julia financial assistance.

Julia turned her down, writing that

> If I honestly felt more money freedom would make my work much better, I would be tempted to accept your offer—but I am sure it has not been the physical work which has been or will be the hardest part for I am used to that and strong, but rather the months of striving against homesickness and the nervous strain of examinations.... Now my brother [Avery] is here, and a place is won at the Beaux-Arts, really mine now it seems, the work might simply be a pleasure whether housekeeping or study. I will thank you for them [your kind words] always.

When Avery arrived in Paris two years after Julia, the two siblings shared an apartment. Avery worked temporarily in an atelier while Julia immersed herself in school work. Her classes, which were taught in French, gave her a vast knowledge of classical architecture to go with her engineering background from the University of California.

In two years, she completed the course requirements, doing better than the school average. Less than a month before her 30th birthday, Julia entered her last student architectural competition—designing a palace theater. She was awarded first prize. It gave her enough points to earn the Ecole des Beaux-Arts certificate, the first ever granted to a woman.

One of the first projects Julia had been commissioned to design was the bell tower, "El Campanil," for Mills College, Oakland.

THREE

Getting Started
1902-1906

As the transcontinental train sped west, Julia longed for the sight of California's golden hills—for a glimpse of the Pacific Ocean. It was hard to believe it had been six years since she and Jessica had left for France. She tried to picture her family. Sam was a young man now. Emma was married, so was Parmelee. Would her parents have changed much? Julia thought about the gifts she had for everyone, secure in the bottom of her trunk.

Had she made a mistake in turning down Pierre's job offer to join his architectural firm? No! There would be work in California. She skimmed her father's letter to support her convictions. Charles Morgan had written on New Year's Day in 1902. "There are more expensive buildings being constructed in San Francisco than at any previous time. Draftsmen are in great demand. It looks like a boom which will stay for sometime." Who else but Julia Morgan, architect, would build their homes, schools, and churches?

At home, Julia was an instant celebrity. After all, she had broken through barriers on two continents to win her architectural credentials.

She moved back into her bedroom in the family home in Oakland. Her father still commuted by ferry to his San Francisco office during the work week, and her mother was involved with social activities in the community. Emma had finished law school—an education as unusual for a woman at that time as her sister's. She practiced law with her husband, Hart North, and was a member of the Queen's Bench, an association for female lawyers.

In the first few months, friends and relatives tried to shower Julia with welcome back parties. She avoided them as much as possible. When well-meaning friends and relatives dropped hints about marriage, Julia changed the subject. She had other things to think about.

She wanted her own office, and, with her parents' backing, she converted part of the carriage house behind the house into a studio. It was not much at first—a drafting table, a cabinet overflowing with pens, pencils, and sketch pads, and a shelf of her architectural books in a corner.

Word spread quickly that the office of Julia Morgan, architect, was open for business. Julia ignored the mostly negative comments from those who did not know her well. What? An architect who is a woman? Who will hire her?

During the first few months, several of Julia's long-time friends called with small commissions, mostly for houses. Many were childhood friends, now married with children of their own. Some were neighbors. They came from the same well-to-do background as Julia.

Phoebe Hearst also wasted little time in contacting the young architect she had met as a student. Hearst's University

From 1902 to 1904, Julia and her staff worked in an office set up in part of her parents' carriage house.

of California building program—her gift to the university— was underway, headed by John Galen Howard. Also a former student at the Ecole, Howard hired Julia to work for him.

Julia joined the design team for the first building, the Hearst Mining Building. A memorial to Phoebe Hearst's husband, a former U.S. senator and miner who had become a multimillionaire by buying mining land in the West, the building was to look like the California missions with white walls and overhanging, red tile roofs.

When Hearst inspected the Mining Building, she was pleased with what she saw. She told John Howard to find Julia Morgan more work. He made Julia his assistant supervising architect on the next Hearst gift to the campus, an outdoor theater shaped in a semicircle like one in Epidaurus, Greece. He told her that the university planned to hold the graduation ceremony in the Greek Theater in May 1903, just a few months away. The speaker was to be the president of the United States.

Julia knew she had to work fast and not make any mistakes. Early one morning in the office she shared with John Howard at the Berkeley campus, she gathered her staff around

The Greek Theatre at the University of California, Berkeley, was completed by Julia Morgan just before the graduation ceremonies in 1903.

a table and unfurled her preliminary sketches. They would be constructing the first classical open-air theater in the United States, she told them. It would be made of reinforced concrete.

As Julia looked around the room, she saw confusion on her workers' faces. She explained that it was a new technique, first done in England, then France. Concrete is poured over steel rods to form an incredibly strong building, much stronger than one using brick, stone, or iron.

Julia and her employees were too busy to be nervous about their project. They ordered tons of concrete and steel rods to form the stage, columns, and seats for 6,000 people. Every day, they worked long hours to complete the job on time.

While working on the theater, Julia met William Randolph Hearst, Phoebe Hearst's only son. He had come west to visit his mother. Thirty-nine-year-old Will Hearst was tall, blond, and blue-eyed. He owned newspapers in Chicago, New York, and San Francisco.

Much to Julia's surprise, Will Hearst knew a lot about architecture and he, too, loved the California landscape. Julia and Hearst talked about their common interests. Before he returned to New York to be married, he told Julia he would have a commission for her later.

Julia did not give it much thought because she was working night and day. After the main pour, when the concrete is poured into large forms, or molds, most of the concrete dried. But the *skene*, the thick wall behind the stage, was still wet. As graduation approached, Julia came up with a plan. She passed out designs for canvas banners to her employees. She told them to sew them up as quickly as possible, then drape them on the wall behind the stage.

When President Theodore Roosevelt gave the graduation address, the concrete was still damp behind the colorful banners. Few people knew the real story. Instead, they complimented Julia on her work.

But she was off on another project. Mills College of Women in nearby Oakland also wanted to begin a building program, starting with a bell tower.

Julia explored the campus and decided to put the tower on a grassy oval where the students would see it when they first came on the campus. Nearby oak and eucalyptus trees would highlight the natural setting. She constructed a 72-foot (22-meter)-high bell tower with a red tile roof and natural gray concrete walls, which were reinforced with steel.

Reviewers raved about Miss Morgan's "gem of a tower." The school newspaper reported that "those who have been privileged to see [the tower and library] are much impressed by the architectural and artistic skill displayed by this lady."

Unspoiled by her success, Julia regularly sought advice from Bernard Maybeck. She found him experimenting by turning houses wrong side out. He did this by drawing support beams on the outside of houses. Inside, beams crisscrossed the open attic area. Julia was upset when some people ridiculed his unusual designs. But his style of architecture was growing popular with homeowners, including Phoebe Hearst.

In 1902, Phoebe Hearst commissioned Maybeck to design a vacation estate for her. She had purchased about 80 forested square miles (207 square kilometers) on the McCloud River, near the Oregon and California border, shadowed by Mount Shasta. Maybeck asked Julia Morgan to assist him.

In Maybeck's studio, the two architects sketched and exchanged ideas for days. Sometimes, Maybeck liked to sit outside and draw under a redwood tree so that he could be inspired by nature. He and Julia came up with a plan for a seven-story medieval Gothic castle constructed of native rock.

Phoebe Hearst's castle at Wyntoon was designed by Bernard Maybeck in 1902. It burned down in 1930.

The estate was called Wyntoon, a Native American name for the area.

Maybeck always loved Wyntoon and wrote "of the river in the foreground roaring ceaselessly, and . . . at the dawn of day, an enchanted castle . . . [with] unobstructed archways . . . tapestries, the little flicker of the fire . . . aged pines, rocks, cascades, great trees fallen years ago—a dishevelled harmony."

Phoebe Hearst was also pleased with Wyntoon and recognized Julia's role in the design. Hearst told Julia that she wanted her to do some more work. She took Julia to see an unfinished hunting lodge on 2,000 acres (810 hectares) out beyond Oakland that had belonged to her husband.

She and Julia took a carriage south on a winding dirt road. Grassy hills and open land stretched in every direction. Cattle roamed the hillsides. Julia saw a few lone houses. She suspected they were *ranchos*, or ranches, from the days when Mexico and Spain controlled much of California and the land was carved into huge cattle ranches.

NE INCH   H   A   C   I   E   N   D   A   D   E   L

They toured the hunting lodge. Hearst told Julia she wanted the lodge remodeled and made into her permanent home. It had to be big enough for her to entertain her family and friends, plus be a place where she could hold functions for all her charity work. The estate would be called the Hacienda del Pozo de Verona—the name referred to a huge Italian stone wellhead that was to go in the gardens.

Julia knew this would be no ordinary house, but a social center. She was familiar with Hearst's charitable works at the University of California and around the country. Hearst cofounded the General Federation of Women's Clubs and the Parent-Teacher Association (PTA), supported the Young Women's Christian Association (YWCA), and worked to restore historical buildings, such as George Washington's home, Mount Vernon.

As they walked and talked that day, Julia pulled a sketch pad from her suit pocket. Quickly, she drew the lodge, changing the roofline until it resembled a multi-level mansion.

O   D   E   L   V   E   R   O   N   A   ELEVATION S

Hacienda del Pozo de Verona, Phoebe Hearst's estate in Pleasanton, California

What about guest houses? Or a swimming pool? She added covered porches and lush tropical plants.

Hearst liked Julia's ideas. She wanted servants' quarters too, plus guest apartments, but she preferred an indoor pool. Julia penciled in the additions. She made a note to herself to review Spanish architecture in her library.

Back in Julia's studio in her parents' carriage house, she drew many of the interior and exterior details. She hired several assistants. Now, her studio looked more officelike, with Julia and her new employees busy at their drafting tables. The smell of polished leather mingled with India ink.

Julia personally inspected every detail of construction. At night, long after her workers had gone home to their families, she polished the final drawings in the carriage house.

Julia spent several years on the Hacienda complex. When it was finished, Phoebe Hearst had a mansion similar to the first sketch Julia had shown her. It looked like a Spanish *presidio*, or fortified settlement. In all, the Hacienda had 92 rooms, including several garages, a bowling alley, tennis courts, a banquet room, a music room, and a ballroom.

As Julia worked on the Hacienda and other projects, she was eager to leave John Galen Howard's employment and work entirely on her own. Although she could have worked at the university or joined the staff at the new School of Architecture, Julia wanted to head her own office. The carriage house was not a real office and it seemed cramped. When a story surfaced that Howard was boasting to his colleagues that he had a wonderful designer, "to whom I have to pay almost nothing, as it is a woman," Julia stepped up her search.

But first, in 1904, Julia took the state examination for certification as an architect. The test was both oral and written, and Julia submitted some of her drawings as part of the process. She passed and became the first woman to be licensed as an architect in California. Later that year, more than two years after returning from France, she moved into a small office on Montgomery Street in San Francisco.

Many San Francisco Bay Area architects called on Julia Morgan in her new office, but not John Galen Howard. He never forgave her for going out on her own. For many years, he used his influence as the supervising architect of the University of California building program to bar her from making any important contributions to the campus.

Two years after she opened her office, the 1906 earthquake struck San Francisco and destroyed Julia's office—right down to the last pencil.

The 1906 San Francisco earthquake, and the fires that followed it, demolished much of the city. This photograph shows the Fairmont Hotel atop Nob Hill with Chinatown in the foreground.

—— ◆ FOUR ◆ ——

An Office of Her Own

1906-1910

At 5:12 A.M., on April 18, 1906, a thunderous boom rocked San Francisco. An earthquake equal to 12 million tons (10.9 million metric tons) of TNT shook the earth again and again. Church bells rang out all over the city. Buildings crashed around the people. When the earth finally stopped shaking, much of the city was a heap of splintered buildings, fallen chimneys, and lifeless bodies.

Fires erupted everywhere, but the fire departments were helpless. Their stations and equipment were either damaged or destroyed. Water lines ruptured; gallons of wasted water flowed into the streets. For days, the city burned unchecked. Fires lit up the skies 50 miles (80 kilometers) away. After the smoke cleared, 700 people were found dead, 300,000 people were homeless, and 28,000 buildings lay in ruins.

People many miles from San Francisco, as well as Julia's parents and others across the bay in Oakland, felt the earthquake and the aftershocks. Many buildings fell in Oakland too. Houses shook, dishes tumbled from cupboards, and windows shattered.

Julia searched helplessly through the rubble that had once been her office. Everything was gone—her books, typewriters, records, drawings. Luckily, her office was small and she had left most of her architectural books at home in Oakland—they were undamaged.

Within a few days, San Franciscans talked about re-building their city. Architects, with or without offices, were desperately needed. And that included Julia Morgan.

In those early weeks, Julia worked night and day. She found time to write Lucy and Pierre LeBrun that everyone in the family was safe. Pierre was shocked at her description of "vacant sites, displaced foundations, shifted paving lanes and stones, not sufficient water to make mortar for bedding for new footing." At times, her task seemed nearly impossible.

The Fairmont Hotel, which sat high above the city of San Francisco on Nob Hill, was nearly complete when the earthquake struck. It was a 600-room Italian Renaissance masterpiece with stately columns inside and out and a grand walkway that overlooked the city. The builders envisioned a grand hotel that would be the fanciest place in the world.

In the 24 hours following the quake, fires finally reached the damaged Fairmont Hotel. Fifteen minutes after the first flames appeared on the ground floor, the hotel was destroyed. All that remained was a granite shell.

A few months after the earthquake, the owners of the Fairmont, the Law brothers, decided they could afford to rebuild the burned-out hotel. They called on Julia Morgan. The Law brothers told Julia that they would like to hire her to rebuild the Fairmont as quickly as possible. They would like to open in a year.

By April 1907, exactly one year after the earthquake, Julia Morgan had completed the reconstruction of the Fairmont Hotel.

Julia was not surprised by their offer.

Since the earthquake, everyone had been talking about her work with reinforced concrete. Word spread quickly that her bell tower on the Mills College campus and her University of California buildings had withstood the earthquake.

For Julia, this was the most important commission of her career so far. She was confident she could handle the work and told the Law brothers that she would take the job—if they could just find her a place where she could sketch.

Everyone, including Julia, knew that the Law brothers were making a daring choice in hiring her. Not only were they offering the job to an architect who had been in private practice only a few years, but to a woman. Yet no one else had her expertise in using reinforced concrete.

Julia accepted the challenge and moved into a temporary office, a rat-infested shack behind the Fairmont. Her desk and drafting table became a rough slab of wood on four legs.

Immediately, she laid out a step-by-step rebuilding plan. She told her staff, "Think it out at the start and finish everything as you go along."

In just 60 days, 121 crippled column sections were replaced. Twisted steel girders, the horizontal beams that held up the ceilings, were either replaced or reinforced. During the following months, stairs and skylights were installed, as was a garden and grand stairway. Rooms and hallways took shape again.

Julia participated in every phase, whether big or small. She thought nothing of climbing rickety scaffolding in what she always wore to work, tailored dark suits and French silk blouses.

One of her chief architect/engineers, Walter Steilberg, described Julia one day as she came down a ladder.

> When she reached the floor (her neat gray suit all dusty and spattered with mortar and her wide-brimmed hat over one ear) she was quite a-glow with enthusiasm with [what she had seen]. . . . She urged me to go up on the scaffold and see for myself. It was a fearful experience; but I went, conquering my trembling.

Her appreciation for quality won Julia the loyalty and admiration of the men and women who worked for her. When a reporter came to inspect the Fairmont, she asked the foreman, "Is the building really in the charge of a woman architect?" The foreman said, "This building is in charge of a *real* architect and her name happens to be Julia Morgan."

Their respect was edged with fear because Julia was a real perfectionist. Once, when Julia inspected some tile work, she did not like what she saw. Amazed workmen watched her rip out the tiles with her bare hands. She told them that the work did not meet her standards. Some of these tiles had nicks. She never spared herself when quality was the issue.

She did not mince words either. When a talented young drafter drew a staircase that was impossible to climb, she called him aside. "Well, young man," she said, because she never remembered names, "I can't deal with fiction writers."

In April 1907, the Fairmont Hotel opened its doors with a banquet for the most distinguished people in the city. It was the largest affair of its kind ever held on the Pacific Coast, and celebrated the rebirth of the city. Fifty cooks and 150 assistants prepared 13,000 oysters, 1,500 chickens, 2,000 loaves of bread, and thousands of small tarts.

After that, the hotel became the city's social center. It also became home for many of San Francisco's wealthiest families, still without permanent shelter after the earthquake and fire.

A *San Francisco Call* newspaper reporter interviewed "Miss Morgan" about the Fairmont. Standing beside Julia in the beautiful ivory, gold, gray, and scarlet dining room, she gushed, "How you must have reveled in this chance to squeeze dry the loveliest tubes in the whole world of color."

Julia answered, "I don't think you understand just what my work here has been. The decorative part was done by a New York firm. My work has been all structural."

Julia vowed never to let this happen again. From then on, she granted interviews rarely, wrote few papers, no books, and entered no architectural competitions.

Julia had no patience with what she called "going around and patting yourself on the back." Although she had confidence in her architectural abilities, she was still reserved. She shunned publicity for the rest of her life.

Over the next few years, San Francisco's skyline slowly reappeared. The new buildings were more earthquake-proof and modern, of concrete and steel. Gone were the gaudy, bawdy, gold-rush era buildings.

Julia reopened her office in the Merchant Exchange Building in San Francisco. A high-rise built in 1903, it had withstood the earthquake. Julia's suite was on the 13th floor and became her office for the rest of her career.

When the Merchant Exchange was first built, traders drove their horse-pulled wagons onto the main floor of the building. The wagons overflowed with grain, hay, gold, and marine equipment which were bartered or traded for other goods.

Julia participated in the remodeling of the interior of the Merchant Exchange Building later on. The original wagon room became a maritime center where ship captains bargained at massive tables. She commissioned William Coulter to paint five 6 x 18-foot (2 x 5-m)-high oil paintings of ships. Other details, such as carved wood ceilings and marble columns, reflected Julia's Beaux-Arts education.

When guests or clients arrived at Julia's office, she ushered them into her favorite room, the library, which had bookcases all around the walls. A table in the center of the room was stacked with huge, leather-bound books. Many came from Pierre LeBrun, who had shipped his collection to Julia when he retired. Everyone in the office was expected to use the library. Over 500 books were available to study; many from Julia's days in Paris showed European architecture.

Next, clients toured the large drafting room. In it stood long, broad tables around which the designers worked. Final

Julia Morgan designed the Methodist Chinese Mission School in San Francisco.

drawings were made using India ink on paper made of linen soaked with starch.

In one corner, Julia had her own high-back desk at which she sketched or consulted her drafters. Her first drawings were usually eight-inch (20-cm) sketches with perhaps a little color. Her employees learned to interpret these sketches and make final drawings. They also drew full-size, large scale details, of everything from wall molding to lighting fixtures.

Julia would stop her clients before a bulletin board covered with photographs of architectural work in progress. She might point to a house being constructed in the mountains near the coast and note the *Arts and Crafts* style, a woodsy style allowing the house to blend in with the natural environment. Or she might point to a photograph of a huge mansion that was to take up an entire city block in which almost every room had to have a view of the Pacific Ocean.

Models of more buildings covered a nearby table. She might show her clients the plans for the Methodist Chinese Mission School in San Francisco or a clubhouse under construction in Los Angeles.

Julia took some of her clients up on the roof of the Merchant Exchange Building to show them the lengthy process necessary to produce copies of the architect's plans. *Blueprints*, or copies, were made by placing the final drawings on a frame over the top of a piece of chemically-treated paper. The sun turned the paper underneath blue except where the original India ink lines were drawn.

Finally, Julia would take her clients into her small office, the size of a cubbyhole. She would close the door and ask, "How can I help you?"

Over the next few years, Julia completed work at Mills College and at the Berkeley campus of the University of

The Kappa Alpha Theta sorority house, designed by Julia Morgan in 1908, was renovated by Julia about 1930.

California. Her only enemy was John Howard, who kept her from any new University of California projects for the next 25 years.

That did not stop her college sorority, Kappa Alpha Theta, from offering her work. The sorority wanted its headquarters near the campus. Julia accepted the commission and designed a redwood-shingle building. The local newspaper read:

HANDSOME NEW HOME FOR
KAPPA ALPHA THETA
A large force of workmen are at work building the first University of California Greek letter sorority clubhouse ever erected by a local chapter in Berkeley.

For six years, Ira Hoover, who had worked with Julia on the Hearst Mining Building, was her junior partner. In 1910, Hoover moved east. The nameplate on the Morgan office door was changed to "Julia Morgan, Architect."

During the rest of her career, Julia ran her office by herself. She never had a problem finding work and all of it was varied.

Julia Morgan designed a playhouse in San Luis Obispo for the daughters of the taxi driver who drove her to and from San Simeon.

FIVE

The Client's
Architect

1907-1913

Julia turned 35 in 1907. At that time, only a handful of women were architects and they had to work full time to succeed in a career dominated by men. If Julia dreamed of marriage and children, she never talked about it.

Julia lived simply at home with her parents and brothers. She and her mother continued to have a strong relationship. Julia looked after Avery. Although he had graduated from college and studied architecture in Paris, he had little ambition. Instead, Avery was "dreamy" and was happy doing odd drafting jobs in his sister's office.

Her brother Sam was everyone's favorite. After high school, he started a moving and storage company. Julia designed a warehouse for him. Later, he joined the Oakland Fire Department.

Julia and her sister remained close friends, in spite of the differences in their personalities. Emma was bubbly and outgoing. She loved clothes and loved being around people.

Julia often visited Emma and her husband, Hart North, in nearby Berkeley. She especially wanted to spend time with her only nephew, Morgan, a blond-headed, happy child.

Spending the holidays with her family was important to Julia. She always participated in Thanksgiving and Christmas get-togethers. Even so, one relative recalled that Julia could not handle a lot of family chatter. Before they knew it, she would be thumbing through a book on art or architecture—or drawing ideas on a scrap of paper.

Julia with her niece, Judith Morgan (Parmelee's daughter), and nephew, Morgan North

Julia's staff became an extension of her family. She was especially fond of the children of her staff members, and she sent them presents at Christmas.

When her secretary, Lillian Forney, had a daughter, Julia followed the baby's development closely and even agreed to become Lynn's godmother. By the time she reached grade school, Lynn often stopped in the office on her way home from school. She recalled one of many times when "Miss Morgan" called to her to come in and say hello.

Lynn tiptoed in. "Miss Morgan" was back to designing a stained-glass window, her fingers smudged with colored chalk. Lynn stood quietly for several minutes, because she knew "Miss Morgan" had forgotten she was there.

Morgan North

Finally, Julia remembered Lynn and showed her the sketch.

"When I was your age," she told Lynn, "I went to a Baptist church across the street from my house. I loved the way the sunlight came through the stained glass windows. That's why I sometimes put these windows in my buildings."

She pointed to a small, elaborately carved box on her desk. "Help yourself while I talk to your mother, then I want to hear about school."

Lynn lifted the lid of the box, then picked a piece of candy. She overheard Julia whispering to her mother, "Make sure you keep the box full of candy while I'm out of town next week. I don't want Lynn or the other children to be disappointed."

From the beginning of her career, Julia designed houses from cottages to mansions. Her first commissions came from "her friends in her youth. She knew them and they knew her and the type of surroundings they wanted to be in." Everyone said she was a "client's architect" because she built for the client, not herself. She had no artistic ego, but let the clients determine what the house would look like. Believing that one should build from the inside out, Julia had her clients visit her office, where they would pore over her books for ideas. They would tell her what they liked and what they did not like.

Next, she would visit the family, often sitting on the floor with the children, to get to know each family member. She always built something special for the children in the house. One house had a hidden closet, another had some secret steps. Julia wanted the children to remember their childhoods as happy times.

One of the many houses designed by Julia Morgan

She tried to match each house to its site. If the land were dry and barren, she might suggest to the client that the house be built in the *California Mission* style with cool tile floors, arches to let the air circulate, and overhanging roofs to block out the sun. She also liked the *Mediterranean* style, where every room opened onto a central patio. The *Arts and Crafts* style, light-filled homes using natural woods, was also popular in the rolling hills of the San Francisco Bay Area.

At the building site, Julia "would come over and talk with the clients with a bunch of old envelopes in her pocket, and she'd make sketches and what not, and go back [to the office] and emerge with the preliminary plans."

When she was not pleased with a drawing, she would tell a worker to go find "Mr. Maybeck," who often used her office. "See if you can't get a little more of the feeling of Maybeck in it," she suggested.

Over the years, Julia constructed homes of all sizes on the coast, in the cities, foothills, and in the mountains. She took from all kinds of styles, and as a result, her houses had a Julia

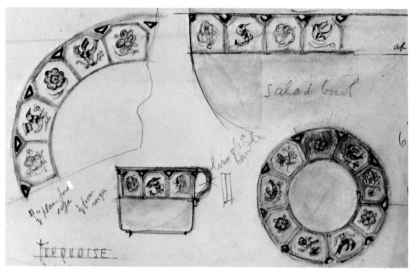

Julia sketched designs for the china to be used at the Berkeley Women's City Club.

Morgan stamp but not a style. They were very balanced-looking. The door was always in the center of the entrance and windows were evenly spaced from one another; everything was in proportion to everything else. The houses had a light and airy outdoorsy feeling, with lots of windows, courtyards, and open porches.

Julia worked hard to perfect every detail. She did this by supervising every step of construction and by hiring the most talented craftspeople she could find. They did wood carving, iron work, weaving, tile work, painting, stone casting, and ornamental plastering—all from full-scale drawings Julia had done herself or approved. If the clients wanted them, Julia designed wood paneling, furniture, dishes, utensils, linens, and lighting fixtures.

Her houses pleased the new owners, and the new owners told their friends and acquaintances. Her reputation grew.

It was not long before Julia was running one of the most prestigious architecture offices on the West Coast. At the time, it was also the largest in the United States headed by a woman. Only 12 years after returning from Paris, Julia had completed more than 300 commissions.

Although she shunned the label "woman architect," Julia was the choice of prominent women such as Phoebe Hearst and the organizations they supported. Whether she liked it or not, her career was intertwined with the new role of women in work and society. Her career was also influenced by changes in the early years of the 20th century. Americans were moving into the cities. Parents wanted more for their children and that included giving them a better education.

Philanthropists like Phoebe Hearst gave large donations of money to help give every child a chance to go to school. She sponsored school building programs across the nation and, at the same time, continued to sponsor Julia Morgan.

Time and time again, Julia was commissioned to build new schools. Her favorite style showed a Mediterranean influence, in which the buildings wrapped around a courtyard. She told her staff to make sure that each classroom had a door leading directly outside.

Julia did not want her schools to have long hallways or winding staircases. She remembered her childhood desire to race outside as quickly as possible to play with her brothers. She wanted every child to get out into the fresh air as soon as possible.

Church construction increased too. Julia received commissions as she always had, through friends, previous clients, and through the craftspeople she knew.

Julia's skill in understanding her clients' needs continued to be a factor. She designed churches for many faiths and ethnic groups, from Swedish Americans to Chinese Americans. Again, she did her homework first, by listening to the church officials, viewing the building site, asking about budgets, and learning about the church's philosophy.

In 1908, Julia was hired to build Saint John's Presbyterian Church in Berkeley, California. This was to be a neighborhood church and Sunday school building on a small budget.

For days Julia thought about how the church should be constructed. When she had a plan she gathered her designers around a drafting table. She showed them a photograph of the building site which dipped slightly towards San Francisco Bay.

It had been a dilemma, she admitted, to come up with a design for the church. They could spend up to two dollars per square foot—and that was not much.

Saint John's Presbyterian Church

Everyone agreed. It was practically impossible, they thought, on that kind of budget.

Julia announced that, as Mr. Maybeck might say, drawbacks could sometimes be turned around into opportunities.

She unfurled some sketches. The church she had designed was a one-story redwood building meant to blend in with the neighborhood. Landscaping and walkways would add warmth. They would be building the Sunday school first. A year later, they would add the church and connect both buildings by tying in the roof line.

Next, Julia uncovered drawings of the inside of the church. They could save money inside. Julia wanted the interior walls, like the exterior, paneled in natural redwood. It was the cheapest and most available kind of wood. Overhead in the ceiling would be wooden beams and supports that

everyone could see. Nuts and bolts would hold the crosspieces together and all would contribute to the overall design.

Julia pointed to another drawing. She had put in high *clerestory* windows, or windows above a lower roofline, of smoked glass on all four walls, so light would filter in from every direction. She had also designed wooden church pews. She explained that the floor needed to slope slightly. That way the worshipers could easily see the clergy and altar at the front of their church.

Julia's employees just shook their heads. Once again, J.M., as they often called their boss, had done it. They knew they would be constructing an architectural masterpiece, well within the church's budget.

When Julia built the church, she also thought about the *acoustics*, the building's qualities that determine whether sounds are clear or not. Because of her acoustically sound design, the minister's voice carried to every corner and the choir filled the sanctuary with sound. Saint John's Presbyterian Church has since become a music center and community theater.

Julia could have turned down this commission and many others. She had plenty of work. But that was not her philosophy. As she told one architect before he left her office to go into private practice, "Don't ever turn down a job because you think it's beneath you. One of the smallest jobs I ever had was a little two-room residence in Monterey [, California]. The lady...was most pleased with the job and [is] now chairman of the YWCA [Young Women's Christian Association]." One small job had led to many large YWCA jobs.

Julia Morgan designed YWCAs that were built up and down the West Coast and from Utah to Hawaii. This is the courtyard of the Honolulu YWCA.

Natural light shines through the large windows to light the stairway in the Residence YWCA in San Francisco.

SIX

Making a Lasting Mark
1913-1919

Julia was excited that childhood friends, family friends, and those who knew her work were seeking her out for a variety of building projects. She could barely wait to get to the office—to pull out a pad and start sketching.

Between six and ten people worked for Julia in her San Francisco office. She had other employees—engineers, contractors, and craftspeople—who were out at the various sites. The employees were on a first-name basis with each other, but they called their boss "Miss Morgan" or "J.M."

Over the years, Julia hired several women for drafting. Others were employed as artists. Most were young and single. Julia was always looking for someone with the same drive and determination as herself, as a possible successor, but she never found that person. Meanwhile, she quietly helped architectural students with college expenses.

It was not easy working in the Morgan office. The problem, said a friend, was Julia, who "thought nothing of working eighteen hours a day [six days a week]." Although she appeared frail, she was "as strong as an ox" and charged through the day on black coffee and chocolate bars. Architect Dorothy Coblentz, who worked for Julia before and after her marriage, recalled that Miss Morgan "didn't realize that people had private lives, that most of the men in the office were married, that there were wives waiting at home for them."

Yet her employees respected her. One man said, "She was . . . quiet in her manner. She never raised her voice or got angry, but she was very particular in her work. She was demanding and everything had to be right; but she did it in a ladylike manner." Everything she did was a team effort. She never said "I," it was always "We."

Dorothy Coblentz added that, "To work with her was to learn [architecture] from the ground up . . . you couldn't put your pencil down unless it meant something. . . . Anyone that had been trained at Julia Morgan's office was welcome at any other office because probably nobody else would have taken the time or trouble to give such a thorough training."

In 1913, while Julia was enjoying her career, tragedy struck. Her 26-year-old brother Sam was riding on a fire truck when it brushed against a concrete wall. He was killed instantly.

The family plunged into mourning. As was the tradition, Eliza Morgan donned somber black clothes and cut back on her social commitments. Charles Morgan reacted differently. To lessen the pain, relatives remembered that he traveled a great deal "out promoting something or other . . . he was more of an outgoing person." Forever optimistic, Charles continued to chase every get-rich-quick scheme that came along.

Since her return from Paris, Julia had developed a close relationship with her youngest brother. Now he was gone, and

Eliza Morgan, left, *dressed in mourning for her son, Sam, and Charles Morgan,* right, *at his office*

Julia could hardly believe it. To relieve her grief, she sketched plans for a tomb to go over his grave, but it was never erected. Instead, in Sam's memory, Eliza Morgan had her daughter design the entrance gate to the Kings Daughters Home, an Oakland hospital that Julia had previously constructed.

During the months following Sam's death, Julia worked hard. She had plenty to do. Her desk was piled high with commissions—about half were from women. Julia was part of the women's movement even though she did not call herself a *suffragist,* or an advocate for women's rights, as did many women.

Many of Julia's clients were independently wealthy women; many were working women. They wanted their own clubhouses, more hospitals, and orphanages. Throughout the 1800s and into the early 1900s, women had united to fight slavery, to repeal the sale of alcohol, and to give women the right to vote. They supported women who became doctors, lawyers, teachers, and architects such as Julia Morgan.

As a result of the women's movement, Julia was commissioned to build a national chain of YWCAs. The directors wanted to provide shelter for young women who were coming into the fast-growing cities to take low-paying factory and city jobs. These new arrivals sought safe, inexpensive, temporary homes. Julia wanted to help. She remembered her penny-saving days on the Left Bank in Paris.

One YWCA, to be built in San Francisco, created quite a stir among board members. At a board meeting, Julia tacked up her drawings and picked up a pointer. "I found that we have a little extra space here . . . my idea is to have one or two little private dining rooms with little kitchenettes so that the girls can invite their friends, and cook a little meal."

The Board opposed it. "These are minimum wage girls there. Why spoil them?"

In her quiet voice, Julia said, "That's just the reason."

A Board member recalled the meeting. Miss Morgan "wanted . . . to have a room where the girls could do sewing, have a sewing machine, and have a little beauty parlor, and could do their laundry. . . . The next time that we were together she planned these rooms. . . . She just quietly did what she wanted to do. And so she had this great success."

Part of her success came from the continual support of Phoebe Hearst, a long-time patron of the YWCA. In 1913, Hearst felt it was time for a conference center to be built in the West. She donated 30 acres (12 hectares) of coastland near Monterey, California, and asked Julia to be the architect.

Light floods through the skylight into the interior of the Oakland YWCA.

Julia first explored the site. Standing on the sand, she watched the crashing surf. Seaweed and saltwater smells filled the air. Julia knew that the conference center should blend in with the coast and the wind-swept Monterey pines and redwoods behind her. From the oversized pockets of her navy suit, she pulled out a small pad and pencil. Julia sketched a low, one-story main building with a stone foundation and redwood walls.

She took her ideas back to her office in the Merchant Exchange Building. She told her drafters that she had some beginning ideas. She wanted to make the center a retreat where members could rest and renew their spirits. The natural setting should be disturbed as little as possible.

From these simple drawings came the first of many buildings at the conference center, named Asilomar, a joining of two Spanish words meaning "refuge by the sea." Stone gateposts marked the entrance. Inside the main building, the walls were unpainted wood; huge beams crisscrossed the ceiling. On foggy days, visitors clustered around a floor-to-ceiling, rough stone fireplace.

Conference attendees leave Crocker Dining Hall at Asilomar after a meal.

The tent houses, above, *and the Phoebe Apperson Hearst Administration Building,* below, *blend in with the environment at Asilomar.*

Merrill Hall, right, *which serves as the auditorium, and the Administration Building,* above, *at Asilomar*

The chapel at Asilomar blends in with the landscape.

YWCA members loved Asilomar. One wrote Phoebe Hearst that "Miss Morgan is A-1, and she is sparing no pains to give us the greatest possible result for the least expenditure."

Over the years, Asilomar grew. Julia constructed a chapel, a kitchen, and a dining hall. She completed other buildings, including a visitor's lodge, with sleeping porches held up by stone pillars.

As a result of the success of Asilomar, everyone connected with the YWCA in the West, and even nationally, became familiar with Julia Morgan, architect. For many years, her

The interior of the chapel at Asilomar

office would design and construct YWCAs across the western United States.

Julia visited Asilomar frequently to supervise the ongoing construction. In March 1919, she wrote Phoebe Hearst. "Yesterday, I returned from Asilomar.... It reminded me... of... the thread of your kindness since those Paris days when you were so beautifully kind to a most painfully shy and home sick girl."

It was their last correspondence. A few weeks later, Phoebe Hearst died at the age of 77 from Spanish influenza, a world-wide flu epidemic that claimed half a million lives in the United States alone. Not only had Julia lost her benefactor and friend, but earlier that year, her mother, Eliza Morgan, had suffered a major stroke.

The month that Phoebe Hearst died, her only child, William Randolph Hearst, came to call on Julia in San Francisco. Architect Walter Steilberg overheard a conversation between the two. "I was at my table, after five o'clock.... I heard this voice, which I had heard before, but I didn't realize what a high pitch Mr. Hearst's voice had. For such a large man, it seemed to me his pitch was very high, so it carried."

Hearst told Julia, "I would like to build something up on the hill at San Simeon. I get tired of going up there and camping in tents. I am getting a little old for that. The other day I . . . was prowling around second-hand bookstores . . . and I came upon this stack of books called *Bungalow Books*."

He showed her a drawing. "I saw this one . . . it gives you an idea of my thought about the thing, keeping it simple."

Hearst wanted Julia to build a small vacation house on part of an old Mexican land grant his father had purchased in 1865. The land, within view of the tiny fishing village of San Simeon, was in a stretch of wilderness in the Santa Lucia Mountains 200 miles (322 km) south of San Francisco.

For years, Will Hearst had enjoyed the outdoor life at San Simeon with his wife, Millicent, and their five sons. They camped on the property in a tent village. Servants erected tents for sleeping, dining, and storage, plus tents for the children's tutors. The main tent was "a great circus tent with a board flooring covered with soft warm rugs."

The next day, Steilberg sketched something for Miss Morgan. But as he recalled later, "it quickly became apparent that Mr. Hearst wanted something grand." An avid art collector, he wanted a place to show off his possessions.

From that point, Julia Morgan and William Randolph Hearst worked together for 30 years to produce the most fabulous "house" in the world at the time.

SEVEN

Building a Dream

1919-1925

After inheriting his mother's money, her fabulous art collection of tapestries, statues, and silver, as well as her property, William Randolph Hearst became one of the richest men in America.

Now, he wanted a place for his own belongings at San Simeon. He owned paintings, ceilings, mantels, panels, stained-glass windows, tile floors, and furniture, many of them purchased from old castles in Europe. He had had his collection dismantled and put into storage.

As early as 1919, Hearst and Morgan realized that a "bungalow" would not house his vast art collection. And perhaps all along, Hearst had dreamed of something much bigger. Julia certainly did and commented to her employees, "I'm building a museum in . . . San Simeon. I'm not building a residence."

To maintain her San Francisco office, Julia commuted to San Simeon on the weekends. For over 20 years, nearly three weekends a month, she left her San Francisco office Friday afternoon and rode the coast train 200 miles (322 km) south to the city of San Luis Obispo. Riding in an upper berth on the train, she sketched during the night on her lap-size drafting table. Next, she took a 50-mile (80-km) taxi ride to Hearst's property with the same driver every week. She worked at San Simeon until Sunday night, then retraced her steps and went directly from the train to her office Monday morning. Between 1919 and 1939, she had made that journey 558 times.

In all the years the two worked together, center stage belonged to William Hearst. Julia's philosophy was to respect the wishes of her client. She supported Hearst's grandiose dreams and said, "If he had chosen that career [of architecture] he would have been a great architect."

Their relationship was both friendly and professional. As was appropriate for the times, they always addressed each other publicly and in letters as "Mr. Hearst" and "Miss Morgan." Biographers would later write that Hearst's mother, Phoebe; his wife, Millicent; his mistress, Marion Davies; and Julia Morgan were equally the most important women in his life.

From the very beginning, Hearst told Julia, "The main thing at the ranch is the view." Architect and client pored over complex plans, working and reworking the details. Millicent Hearst also worked with Julia, and shared much of her husband's enthusiasm for San Simeon in the early years. The Hearsts separated in 1924 and lived apart but never divorced. After that, Will Hearst's constant companion was actress Marion Davies.

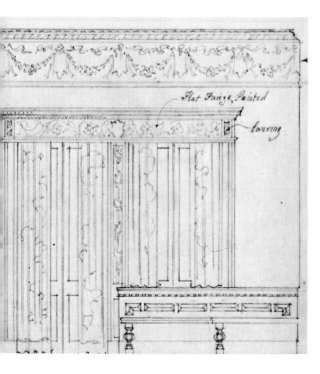

Julia made countless sketches for the guest houses. This is one design for the sitting room of La Casa del Mar.

The final design included a main house, three guest houses, a rose garden, and a pool, all with a view of the Pacific Ocean. The main house, where the Hearst family would live, would be similar to a cathedral he had seen in Spain. Hearst requested that the buildings, gardens, and pools should all be linked by a "plan of walks and flower beds or landscape features . . . that will bring all . . . together into a harmonious whole."

Although the original building site was barren and rocky, William Hearst formally named it "La Cuesta Encantada" in 1924, Spanish for "The Enchanted Hill." But in conversation, Hearst simply referred to the property and the house as "the ranch." Later visitors would call it Hearst Castle, but Hearst did not. He also owned an ancient stone castle in Wales, filled with Medieval armor, which he bought in 1925.

Julia set to work. Drawing on her engineering skills, she created a five-mile (8-km)-long, winding road which snaked up 1,600 feet (488 m) to the mountaintop. First horses and wagons, then trucks, would haul materials to the site. Hearst

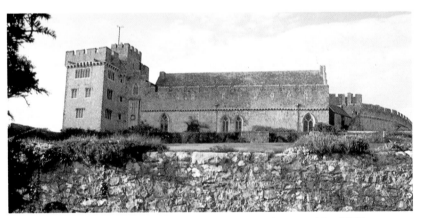

St. Donat's Castle in Wales was another castle owned by William Randolph Hearst.

The beautifully landscaped gardens and pathways frame La Casa Grande.

wrote, "My Dear Miss Morgan: If other trucks are necessary please . . . secure one or two more, and get the kind that will stand up and that are peculiarly adapted to hill climbing."

Below on the shoreline, a wharf was constructed at San Simeon to receive sea shipments. Goods were loaded in the morning in San Francisco or Oakland and arrived in San Simeon 24 hours later. In 1919, Julia wrote, "Dear Mr. Hearst, The *Cleone*, a very disreputable old coaster, sailed . . . for San Simeon, fully insured, with cement, lumber for forms, nails, reinforcing bars for concrete, ready roofing, and a second hand band saw and rock crusher."

From her drafting table flowed designs for warehouses. She included a railroad track so shipments could be easily unloaded and rolled into the warehouses. Julia worried about supplies. "The shortages of every kind of material and workmen out here is incredible, from draughtsmen to window glass." Hearst did not flinch over these and other problems. His response was, "Do what ever is necessary. I'll pay the bills."

Julia signed on construction and warehouse workers. Later, she hired the household staff as well and was responsible for as many as 100 individuals.

It did not take the workers and craftspeople long to learn that "Miss Morgan" was not only fair, but extremely knowledgeable about construction. "She held the artisans who worked on her jobs in high regard, and greatly admired a fine bricklayer, a fine stone mason, or someone else who was very good at his job."

Julia worried about her employees' housing. In the early months of construction, a labor camp of tents popped up next to the tiny town of San Simeon. Later, near the warehouses, Julia designed simple homes with white walls and red tile roofs.

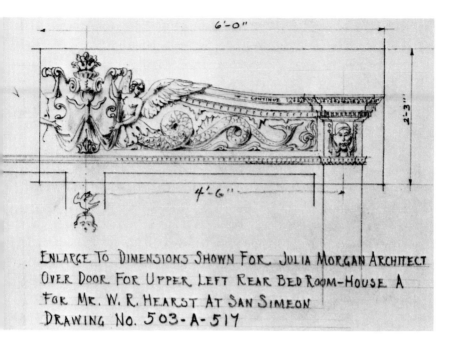

ENLARGE TO DIMENSIONS SHOWN FOR JULIA MORGAN ARCHITECT
OVER DOOR FOR UPPER LEFT REAR BED ROOM-HOUSE A
FOR MR. W. R. HEARST AT SAN SIMEON
DRAWING No. 503-A-517

Julia soon discovered that being a construction boss for such a large group was not easy. Some crew members were unpredictable transients; many found the foggy winters too dreary and isolated, and they returned to the cities. To improve things, she arranged for a cook and a weekly movie. She wrote, "I have tried a moving picture show once a week . . . which has been worth the money in keeping down 'turn-over.' "

Hearst maintained a busy lifestyle. Wherever he was, he sent Julia letters or telegrams with ideas and sketches for changes and additions, including his wife's preferences. These letters and telegrams would number in the thousands and detail the step-by-step construction at San Simeon and later Hearst projects. Julia tried to answer every one.

Back in New York, Hearst toured art galleries, looking for art to add to his collection. The galleries were overflowing

The library

with art, household furnishings, and architectural works of every description from Europe. World War I had ended in 1918, leaving much of Europe in ruin. By 1919, European families were rebuilding their lives by selling their possessions to the highest bidders—often Americans.

Hearst began bidding on art and antiques, spending about one million dollars a year, and stockpiling everything for San Simeon. He hired agents to scour Europe for art treasures. In March of 1920, he sent the first of many freight cars of treasures to San Simeon. Julia had her work cut out for her. Somehow, she had to mix and match architectural parts that spanned 1,000 years. Yet she seemed challenged and wrote,

> So far we have received...some twelve or thirteen carloads of antiques....I don't see myself where we are ever going to use half suitably, but I find that the idea is to try things out and if they are not satisfactory, discard them for the next thing that comes that promises better.

Meanwhile, atop the Enchanted Hill, tons of earth were carted up from the lower meadows for future gardens and

The gothic study

orchards. Water was piped in from mountain springs five miles (8 km) away. The three guest houses were to be built first. They would be below the site for the main house so as not to affect the view.

Before the three guest houses could be built, Hearst ordered workers to move four large oak trees. Pointing to one tree, Hearst said, "I want it moved about a hundred feet that way. And this one I want moved a hundred and fifty feet this way. And I want this one turned so that the big branch comes over the roadway." One tree weighed 600 tons (544 metric tons). Crews extracted the trees, encased their roots in huge concrete tubs, and hoisted them to their new spots.

Julia supervised the construction of the guest houses. Architect Edward Hussey remembered doing a layout for a diamond-patterned marble floor in one house. Miss Morgan "had me make the full-sized layout—about four feet square or so—on tracing paper." She laid it down on the floor of the drafting room. "That was the first time I had seen a drawing walked on to get the feeling of it, but that was what she did in that case."

*One of Julia's
drawings for
a floor tile*

As work continued, Julia was actively involved in all areas of construction, which meant walking the scaffolding to inspect work. Her nephew, Morgan North, recalled that, "she would...go with her hands in her [suit] pockets and looking up above...and she put her hands in with her thumbs sticking out...and every once in a while, when they hadn't fenced off a stairwell or something, she would go right down to the floor below."

Day after day, month after month, the work crept forward, but not without many delays. Hearst himself was a

La Casa del Mar, near right, *and La Casa del Sol* far right, *are under construction. La Casa del Sol after completion,* below

problem. He constantly changed plans and introduced new ideas. In one guest house, he ordered a fireplace moved to another spot in the room. Six months later, he changed his mind and had it rebuilt in the original spot. At times, Julia grew frustrated and impatient. Her love of and ease with children probably helped her understand William Hearst's willful behavior. Julia later said that demolition formed a good part of the project.

Nevertheless, the three guest houses began to take shape. Each had 10 to 18 rooms. They were really mansions in size, with Spanish-style white walls and tile roofs. Each had an entrance hall, a grand sitting room, and fabulous furnishings.

Each guest house had a Spanish name: La Casa del Monte faced the mountains, La Casa del Mar faced the sea, and La Casa del Sol looked toward the setting sun.

The sitting room in La Casa del Mar

After viewing the houses, Hearst wrote Julia on March 18, 1920, "All the little houses are stunning. . . . Please complete them before I can think up any more changes."

By the summer of 1921, the first guest house, La Casa del Monte, was ready for Will and Millicent Hearst. For the five boys, who ranged in age from six-year-old twins to a 17-year-old, their camping days at the ranch were over.

In 1924, the three houses were complete and the main house, La Casa Grande, was under construction. On Christmas Eve of 1925, Hearst hosted a housewarming for the unfinished La Casa Grande.

La Casa Grande

 EIGHT

Hearst's Castle
1920-1928

Julia turned down an invitation to direct the YWCA's world-wide building program because she did not want to be away from her family that much. Her mother had health problems and, in 1923, her father had had a stroke. He now needed constant care. Julia's busy schedule meant she could not tend her father. Neither could Emma, who had her husband, Hart, and young son, Morgan, born in 1914, to care for. Parmelee had died in 1918, leaving a daughter, Judith, who lived in southern California. So the responsibility for their parents fell on Avery, who was unmarried and living at home.

Until his father's death in 1924, Avery provided round-the-clock nursing care. Soon after, Avery suffered a nervous breakdown due to the stress of caring for his father. From then on, Avery became Julia's responsibility. Despite the fact that she did not drive, Julia purchased a Hudson so her brother could be her chauffeur. He continued to do odd jobs at her office as well.

In the mid-1920s, Julia bought a pair of adjoining houses in San Francisco. She remodeled them into apartments and moved into one. She shared everything with her renters—mostly single young women—from food to holidays. One woman reflected that Miss Morgan "always took a great interest in how we decorated our apartments, and while I am sure she did not always think we had the best taste, she never betrayed by the flicker of an eyelash, that she did not entirely agree with what we had done."

Left: *One of Julia's drawings for the west entrance of the main building at San Simeon.* Right: *The west entrance after completion.*

Three times a month, Julia traveled to San Simeon. Construction was at its peak. When the main house was nearly completed, Julia wrote Hearst, "Yesterday, I had a pleasant walk along the...main building roof. The view is *great* and the lovely clear weather allowed one to see way up and down the coast."

In a later visit, Hearst agreed, then casually said, "Build another story. We'll call it the Celestial Suite."

As usual, Julia did not complain. Her role was to fulfill the client's wishes. But an architect from her office did. "It didn't give Miss Morgan a chance to use her real talent. She was like a man playing the piano backwards."

More and more, Hearst stayed at the ranch. He was dazzled with everything and wanted to show it off. Invitations to his house were snapped up by famous people, such as

Movies were shown to Hearst's guests in the screening room at San Simeon.

Calvin Coolidge, Winston Churchill, Charlie Chaplin, Harpo Marx, Cary Grant, Clark Gable, Charles Lindbergh, and Amelia Earhart. Hearst threw costume parties, flew in fresh food from all over the world, staged overnight camping trips, and was forever thinking of new ways to please his guests.

Although Hearst Castle had become the social center of the West, work continued. Julia drew plans for more guest houses. She started construction on a movie theater that would seat 50 in red-velvet armchairs. Eventually there would be 144 rooms at San Simeon, each containing a profusion of objects from almost every century and style.

The sparkling white main building with its twin towers dominated the hill. Carved teak trim and colorful tiles added to the design. A cast-stone balcony crossed the front of the building and outlined the high main story.

Choir stalls and tapestries line the wall to the right of the fireplace in the Refectory.

Inside, guests socialized in the huge two-story Assembly Hall with its 16th-century ceiling and Italian tapestries on the walls. Some 30 guests could dine at a 17th-century Italian table in the Refectory. Twenty-eight feet (9 m) overhead were silk banners and life-size wooden figures of saints. One wall was lined with 500-year-old Spanish choir stalls.

Hearst regularly slipped back to San Simeon to inspect progress and confer with Julia. Few guests noticed the quiet little woman who roamed among them, gray-suited, wearing glasses and no makeup. But one who did notice her recalled a dinner party when Julia sat directly across from Hearst. "They were talking back and forth, and gesturing, and he was drawing things, and she was drawing things. The rest of the guests could have been miles away. They didn't pay attention to anybody."

Julia brought together statuary, landscaping, and the play of light to create the Neptune Pool, above *and* opposite.

Many talented young artists, men and women, earned their reputation with Julia because she encouraged and recognized their skills. In turn, they were fiercely loyal to "Miss Morgan" even after Hearst Castle construction slowed in 1937.

From the beginning, the land surrounding the buildings was part of the overall design. Hearst wanted formal gardens. He ordered thousands of plants and trees. Then he requested a poultry farm, orchards, and vegetable gardens so his guests would have fresh food.

During a 10-year period, Julia supervised the replacing of barren hills with trees and shrubs. Fruit trees thrived in holes blasted in rock and packed with topsoil. Flower beds and lily ponds were everywhere. There were walkways, gardens, ponds, statues, rose beds, hedges, orchards, vegetable beds, and more.

It was common for Hearst to buy something, then tell Julia to use it. When he purchased the front of a Roman temple

*During early construction, the twin towers of La Casa Grande
seemed to rise from the summit of the Enchanted Hill.*

William Randolph Hearst and Julia Morgan confer over blueprints at San Simeon.

with granite pillars, he first wanted it in a garden, then near a reflecting pond. Following his wishes, Julia made dozens of sketches putting the temple near a pond. Hearst changed his mind. Now, he wanted it to go behind a swimming pool.

Julia was challenged. How could she build a swimming pool on the steep hillside site that Hearst had selected? She knew she would find the answer—it would just take her a while to sort through all the possibilities.

Years later, after hundreds of drawings and numerous changes, Julia finished what architects described as "the most sumptuous swimming pool on earth." It was called the Neptune

*The Neptune
Pool, left, and
Roman pool,*
above

This is one of many of Julia's sketches for the entrance to the tennis courts on top of the Roman pool.

Pool, after a legendary god of the sea. Julia supported the outdoor pool with reinforced concrete beams attached to a concrete retaining wall. At the end of the white marble-lined pool stood the ancient and enlarged temple. Dressing rooms were constructed above the pool. During the hot, dry California summers, the Neptune Pool was popular with Hearst and his guests. So was a second, indoor Roman-style pool, lined with blue and gold Italian glass tiles, and located beneath the tennis courts.

Julia, who had spent childhood summers at the seashore, probably never had time to swim. Yet she added changing rooms, beauty salons, and sunbathing areas to the many pools she constructed for Hearst, the YWCA, and various clubs.

In 1924, Hearst acquired 40 Montana buffalo. He decided he wanted a zoo and handed Julia yet another challenge. Over the years, Julia designed closed-in grottoes for the dangerous animals like tigers and bears. She fenced in the estate so that the deer, yaks, emus, and zebras could roam freely. She wrote Hearst that "the animals do look very picturesque and interesting as seen unexpectedly grouped here and there. Now, if you could come on the lions for instance, as unexpectedly, it would produce a real thrill." Eventually, guests would be amused by more than 100 species composing the largest private zoo in the world at the time.

Signs on the estate read, "Animals Have Right of Way." Winston Churchill, Prime Minister of England, once had to wait on the road approaching the houses because a giraffe

Julia feeds "Mary Ann," a member of the menagerie at San Simeon.

rested there. Mice scampered about the buildings; Hearst would not hear of killing them. In fact, guests were forbidden to mention death. William Hearst hated dead leaves or flowers in his garden and had groundskeepers remove them at night by flashlight.

During this heavy period of construction at the ranch, Hearst was the country's most lavish spender. He paid out

By 1930, the recreation wing of La Casa Grande is under construction.

more for housing and decoration than anyone in history. Over the years he would channel millions of dollars into his Enchanted Hill.

An aerial photograph of Hearst's Enchanted Hill shows La Casa Grande on the summit and the Neptune Pool in the foreground.

Julia was the paymaster, but did not always have enough money. In one letter she wrote,

> I have been charging you...6% of the cost of the work....6% does not cover the actual cost expenses. ...You know how I feel about San Simeon and so will understand it is not a question of making a little more or less, but there is a real need not to go behind, and I know you would not want it.

When Hearst was short of cash, he borrowed money from one of his newspapers or sold something from his art collection.

Despite money problems at Hearst Castle, construction continued steadily. Julia had other jobs, other things to worry about, including her mother's deteriorating health. The Oakland neighborhood where Eliza Morgan lived was run down. Eliza refused to move in with either Emma or Julia.

The two sisters devised a plan. With Emma's support, Julia built a house on a lot next to her sister's house, without telling their mother. Morgan North recalled what happened next.

> [Aunt Julia] made a room exactly the same—proportions and fireplace and everything as her room in the old house was. We brought Grandma out on Thanksgiving day for dinner to our house...and then after dinner was over, we had the usual conversation in the living room. They took Grandmother...into the new house. She looked at the downstairs; she didn't recognize it. But the minute she got upstairs, the bed and dressers and all the things were in exactly the same place, and there was the fire in the fireplace. She made no comment whatever—never made any comment about the switch.

The McCloud River rushes by the Cinderella House at Wyntoon.

—⊰⊶ NINE ⦼⊱—

A Fairy-Tale Village

1928-1940

Julia was relieved to have her mother next door to her sister. That way, Emma could visit daily and supervise the nursing staff. Julia told a friend that "my mother is stronger in body and mind...but is confined to bed—or at most a small voyage around her room."

In 1930, Eliza Morgan died and was buried in the Morgan family plot in Oakland, California.

When Julia was in San Francisco, she worked late at night in her office. One employee recalled seeing her so tired her head was on the table from fatigue. But she would be up and at it again. After work, Julia rode the cable car to the end of the line and walked two and a half blocks home.

One of her renters remembered Julia's typical pattern.

> We would hear the front door close very quietly, and soon the fragrance of coffee would assail our nostrils and we knew that Miss Morgan was safely in—and ready for bed after two or three cups of strong, black coffee!

> [Her] interests in life did not include food....
> If left to her own devices, Miss Morgan would open a
> can. To leave something cooking on the stove, was
> fatal for her—as her mind would be on something and
> she...would be recalled by the aroma of burning
> toast, or something scorching in a pan.

Since childhood, Julia had battled ear problems. And even though they were becoming more serious, she told no one. According to Flora North, Morgan's wife, "she would never mention anything physical. In fact there was a family thing not to mention a sickness."

So when Julia had an operation in the early 1930s, her relatives did not find out until afterwards. Her doctor performed an emergency mastoidectomy, the removal of Julia's inner ear. During the surgery, he accidentally severed a facial muscle. As a result, Julia's face sagged on that side, as though she had had a slight stroke.

The doctor never sent her a bill, said her nephew. Julia "realized that in some respects he was more hurt than she was. She used to send a present to him every year at Christmastime...an armload of orchids, because he had said his wife loved orchids."

The mastoid surgery affected Julia's sense of balance. One friend said that she "used to walk a little bent. I've seen her walk...near buildings, and sometimes touch the buildings as she came along." At work, she still climbed ladders and walked scaffolding, but hung onto a worker's pockets.

Despite her health problems, Julia was no invalid. She designed a YWCA in San Francisco's Chinatown, adding touches that were sacred to the Chinese. She wrote Hearst about plans for a Chinese guest house at San Simeon. Her interest in Chinese art had begun during her stay in Paris. Seeing the art in the Trocadero Museum in Paris had given her a new perspective on the Orient. Back home, Julia's fascination with Chinese culture and architecture and with the Chinese who lived in the San Francisco Bay Area continued.

Other projects included the Berkeley Women's City Club, a castlelike, medieval, six-story clubhouse designed around two courtyards and with a large indoor swimming pool. Every detail—including the lighting fixtures, dishes, and linens—was designed by Julia. To make sure the chairs were right, she suggested that members appoint a committee of one tall, one short, and one overweight club member to sit in them.

One of Julia's sketches for the Berkeley Women's City Club

*The Members'
Lounge in the
Berkeley
Women's City
Club*

Although construction had started to slow down, Julia continued to go to San Simeon. But she did not like to see people there. Instead, she hibernated in her office at the ranch and worked night and day. Only her staff knew she was there. She declined to eat in the dining hall with the guests, saying, "The face has not yet regained its normal form. For an architect, it is more or less embarrassing to present so unsymmetrical an appearance!"

While she was working on Hearst Castle, her San Francisco office continued to accept dozens of other commissions.

Julia fishes at Wyntoon soon after her mastoid surgery.

The Honolulu YWCA

From San Francisco, Julia directed the construction of a Honolulu, Hawaii, YWCA complex, using clean beach sand and crushed blue lava rock in the concrete. During the same time, Hearst asked Julia Morgan and Bernard Maybeck to build a women's gymnasium at the University of California on the Berkeley campus. It was to be a memorial to his mother, Phoebe Hearst.

The University of California also honored Julia Morgan. In May of 1929 Julia donned the traditional black robe and mortar-board hat and accepted an honorary degree of Doctor of Laws during graduation ceremonies. Her degree read:

> Distinguished alumna of the University of California; Artist and Engineer; Designer of simple dwellings and stately homes, of great buildings nobly planned to further the centralized activities of her fellow citizens; Architect in whose work harmony and admirable proportions bring pleasure to the eye and peace of mind.

One friend wrote, "When I got a phone call saying . . . have you heard the news? . . . I screamed right out in the telephone booth for sheer happiness." In uncharacteristic behavior, Julia accepted the attention she received from family, friends, and coworkers. She saved her many congratulatory notes.

That October, the New York stock market crashed. Millions of Americans lost money and their jobs, banks closed, and companies shut down. It was the beginning of the Great Depression, which would last several years. At the time, Hearst Castle was the largest private construction project in California. As the depression continued, it caused a crisis in Hearst's publishing business that required him to cut back building programs, including some at Hearst Castle. By the late 1930s, construction at San Simeon ceased. Many unfinished projects remained on the drawing boards, including another wing for La Casa Grande.

A few months after the depression started, Julia decided to take a vacation, something she seldom did. Before leaving she wrote, "Dear Mr. Hearst, Tonight I am leaving for New York—the first trip there since we began on San Simeon [1919]. I am looking forward to the vacation like an infant just out of school. Julia Morgan."

Always an optimist, Hearst continued to bombard his architect with additional plans at other sites even though the ranch was far from complete. He dreamed about a mansion on property he owned on the edge of the Grand Canyon in Arizona. Julia chartered a plane and pilot and flew over the Grand Canyon saying that she wanted to see what it was like up there. She loved both the flight and the aerial view.

Although a cabin was built on the south rim of the Grand Canyon, a mansion never materialized. Yet Julia was far from idle. She designed a hunting lodge for Hearst 30 miles (48 km) from the ranch. Called Jolon, it included a Mission-style main building with apartments for guests. An octagonal dome rose above the second floor.

In 1931, Julia and Emma traveled to Europe. Julia planned to gather ideas for yet another Hearst project, the rebuilding of Wyntoon. The northern California castle that Bernard Maybeck had designed in 1902 had burned to the ground. Hearst wanted another castle with guest houses to hold his collection of Germanic art. He had stone mantels, tapestries, statues, porcelain, antler chandeliers, a fountain from a German castle, and more.

Hearst sent his limousine and chauffeur to meet Julia and her sister in Naples, Italy. The driver was to "take Miss Morgan anywhere in Europe she wishes to go." Emma and Julia drove through German forests and visited Austria. Julia

Hearst originally intended for guests to ride horseback from San Simeon to Jolon Ranch, above, *for an overnight stay.*

sketched medieval mansions and castles. She revisited Paris and toured Spain.

On her return, Julia and her staff began to create a German village for William Hearst. To do this, Julia commuted north to Wyntoon one weekend a month on the train. The trip took all day; a driver took her the rest of the way deep into the forest. Three weekends a month, she traveled to Hearst Castle and worked with Spanish and Mediterranean architecture. Weekdays, she shifted her attention to her other commissions, for colleges, churches, private homes, and YWCAs. This ability to go from project to project reflected Julia's talent: to design for the client, not for herself.

In the pine forest at Wyntoon, Julia constructed three separate three-story cottages named after fairy tales. Bear House, where Hearst lived, had murals on the outside walls from *Grimm's Fairy Tales*. They told the story of Snow White and Rose Red. Murals on the outside walls of the Cinderella House told the story of Cinderella. The third house, Sleeping Beauty—now called Angel or Fairy House—was never completed inside, nor was the main house ever started.

The houses, which looked like miniature castles, circled a grassy clearing in the forest and backed onto the McCloud River. Each had four to eight bedrooms, each with its own bath. Homey touches included armchairs with footstools, reading lamps, writing desks, and baths with river and forest views. Guests enjoyed horseback riding, croquet, tennis, and, at the Gables, a stone and half-timber building, dined and watched movies. Julia constructed a pool of blue-green marble next to the McCloud River. On one end was a manufactured deck of sand—for sunbathing on "the beach."

Despite her physical handicaps, Julia worked on Wyntoon until the 1940s. She trained herself to overcome her ear

Julia made many sketches for Hearst's German village at Wyntoon.

problems and did—almost entirely. Yet her balance was never the same. Occasionally, she fell. Morgan North remembers once at Wyntoon, Julia "was walking down that ditch. . . . she thought the ferns were on solid ground. She stepped over and slid down the bank, and oh, golly, her head was a mass of scars."

Originally called the Sleeping Beauty House, the Angel or Fairy House is nestled among the pines at Wyntoon.

Julia picked herself up and brushed off the weeds. She did not feel sorry for herself—it was not her way. Instead, she loved working, loved being at Wyntoon. Her frequent letters to William Hearst show this enthusiasm. In one note, she wrote that the "tiger lilies [are] out. Wild roses and foliage beautifully clean and fresh from late rains—houses too are cheerful crisp and fresh."

For Julia, going to Wyntoon was a chance to escape into a fairy-tale world. In the real world, war was threatening again in Europe. Money from the Hearst Corporation was dwindling. So were building supplies. And Julia was older.

Emma North, left, *and Flora North,* right, *board the ship in San Francisco before Julia,* center, *leaves on a cruise around South America and to Spain and Portugal.*

TEN

The Last Chapter

1939-1957

In 1939, World War II began in Europe. Many countries— including the Axis powers of Germany, Italy, and Japan, and the Allied powers of France, Great Britain, the Soviet Union, the United States, Canada, India, China, Australia, and South Africa—were eventually involved in the fighting.

Avery died in 1940. For nearly 17 years, Julia had been totally responsible for him. Before that, she had also cared for her parents. Now, for the first time in her life, Julia was without adult companionship. Emma was busy with her family; Parmelee's daughter lived in southern California.

Julia continued to show interest in her friends and her employees, especially their children. She sent engraved silver cups to new babies and ordered children's books in small sizes "to fit their little hands."

Christmas, Easter, and Thanksgiving became more important than ever. A week before Christmas, Julia always got "into the holiday spirit," as one of her renters remembered.

> First were the greens, then the wreaths . . . greens and mistletoe . . . on the mantle . . . [and a] tree for Miss Morgan's living room—and every branch bearing a small white candle—and at the top a silver star.
>
> Slowly, the [tree] would disappear under the mountain of packages which grew as the doorbell would ring and various friends stopped to leave Christmas gifts for Miss Morgan. These came from . . . contractors, workmen, people in her office—people who lived at San Simeon . . . and all who loved her. She was most pleased by some simple gift, made by hand.

Work kept her busy. Like everyone else, she listened to her radio and read her newspaper to keep informed about the war situation. Julia wondered if the United States would get involved.

Then, on December 7, 1941, the Japanese bombed Pearl Harbor in Honolulu, Hawaii. President Franklin D. Roosevelt declared war.

After the Pearl Harbor attack, no one knew where the Japanese might strike next. Fearing that San Simeon might be hit, Hearst moved to Wyntoon. From an office there, he ran his vast newspaper empire and dreamed of new projects, including one in Mexico.

He owned a 1,400-square-mile (3,626-square-km) cattle ranch in Chihuahua in northwestern Mexico. Although there was a 40-room adobe house—Babicora Hacienda—on the property, he wanted Julia to enlarge it.

Julia made several trips to Hearst's Babicora Hacienda, traveling four or five days on Mexican railroads. She drew up plans for a large house, servants' quarters, and a pool. But the new hacienda was never built. Rumors had been flying around that the Mexican government might confiscate property held by foreigners, so the project was put on hold.

In 1943, Hearst wrote Julia, "No one knows how long this war will last. Or how long I will last, for that matter." William Hearst was 80; Julia Morgan was 71.

The war created major labor and material shortages. Julia reduced her staff to a skeleton force. She worried about the young men, sons of employees and friends, who were soldiers in the war. Her nephew, Morgan North, was stationed in the South Pacific.

For the first time, Julia had time for a friend—Flora North, Morgan's young wife. The two women talked for hours around the fire at night. Julia took up her one and only hobby, Chinese calligraphy. The Chinese alphabet includes about 50,000 characters, or word symbols. In order to read Chinese, one must know at least 5,000. To draw Chinese characters, Julia used black ink and a brush. Flora was a potter and studied designs in her aunt's architectural books. Morgan North recalled that, "Flora was privileged to have one of the best relationships with her of anybody I know. Aunt Julia

From top left to bottom right, *Flora North, Sachi Oka, Sally Moon Morgan, Julia Morgan, Emma Moon, Hart North, Emma North, Judith Morgan*

never relaxed at all until the war. . . . she simply could not do the building that she wanted, and she was not about to go out and build war work because this was not her line."

Despite the war, Julia and Hearst dreamed of new ideas. Architect and client visited each other. They planned one last major commission: an art museum for San Francisco. In the early 1930s, Hearst had purchased an enormous Spanish monastery made of stone. The dismantled monastery was brought to San Francisco harbor on 11 ships and stored in a warehouse. Hearst wanted Julia to use it to build an art museum that would be as grand as those in New York.

Julia presented her drawings to city officials. She would reuse the stones and build a medieval-style museum, Julia explained, and reinforce it with steel as protection from California's earthquakes. "Mr. Hearst," she told the city, would donate the materials.

San Francisco set aside some land. But, like Babicora, the museum was never built. A fire, probably arson, damaged the crated material and the city backed away from its original decision. For once, Hearst did not use his influence to push the project through. His health was failing and his sons were becoming more and more involved in the Hearst Corporation. Julia's last big project was not to be.

By 1939, Julia had shifted her attention from San Simeon to Wyntoon, but letters to Hearst showed her concern for the preservation of San Simeon. After the war, construction at Hearst Castle reopened for two years to enlarge the wings of La Casa Grande. In 1947, poor health forced William Hearst to move to Beverly Hills, California, so he could be closer to medical specialists. He died in 1951 at the age of 88.

That same year, Julia decided to close her office in the Merchant Exchange Building where she had been since 1907.

She was 79. Her closest friends were dead; so were many of her clients. Many of her coworkers had gone to other architectural offices. Julia had no one to carry on her practice.

She told a remaining employee that architectural styles were changing, that she disliked the International style with its plain lines and chrome. She would work in any style—Greek, Roman, Italian, Spanish, Mediterranean, Mission, or the woodsy Arts and Crafts style—but not modern.

Julia knew the real reason why she was retiring. Her energy was failing—and her mind. As her niece recalled, "her memory started to become confused and she was aware of it. She was too bright not to know it."

Julia sent postcards to everyone from her file, saying that she was retiring. If anyone wanted drawings back, they should let her know. Otherwise she would destroy them.

After a certain deadline, Julia contacted the building superintendent. Burn my files, blueprints, and records, she told him. My clients have their own copies. She saved her Beaux-Arts drawings and her correspondence with William Randolph Hearst.

Now she had free time. She traveled continuously. Always an architect, she sketched and filled notebooks with ideas. But her travels ended after a freighter trip to Spain and Portugal. At a port stop, she got lost and almost missed the ship. Julia hoped to be lost at sea and told Morgan and Flora, "Maybe sometime when I go on one of these trips, I won't come back."

Back in San Francisco, she was mugged and had to be hospitalized. Frightened by her limitations, Julia hired a nurse-companion to care for her in her apartment. She saw few people and did not leave her bedroom the last four years of her life.

Julia Morgan died on February 2, 1957, when she was 85 years old. As she requested, her burial was "a quick tuck-in with my own."

A month after Julia's death, several friends set up a scholarship fund at the University of California. Today, the money aids architectural students.

Later in 1957, the state of California accepted the San Simeon property as a memorial to William Randolph Hearst and his mother, Phoebe Hearst. This included the buildings, art, 123 acres (50 hectares), and some land at the base of the hill to be used as an entrance way, visitor center, and parking lot.

The property, now known as the Hearst San Simeon State Historical Monument, opened to the public in 1958. Eighteen years later, the Department of the Interior designated it a National Historic Landmark. Restoration and research at Hearst Castle continues. At least one million visitors tour the main building, guest houses, and the grounds each year.

Asilomar is also a California State Monument. It is used as a conference center. Hearst Castle and Asilomar are the biggest money-makers in California's state park system. Wyntoon belongs to the Hearst family.

Until a few years ago, only a handful of people had ever heard of Julia Morgan. Outside her circle of friends and clients, she was unknown—by choice. She never entered competitions, wrote articles, gave interviews, or wrote her memoirs.

Even though she sought anonymity, architectural historians are uncovering more information about Julia Morgan's 47-year career. Over 700 structures bear her name. She worked for individuals and institutions—designed schools, churches, stores, hospitals, houses, swimming pools, YWCAs,

One of Julia Morgan's legacies — Neptune Pool with the twin towers of La Casa Grande at San Simeon in the background

women's clubs, created Hearst Castle, Wyntoon, and much more. Experts rank Julia Morgan as one of America's leading architects.

Her nephew summed up her success. "She had a brilliant mind, a few words and she'd understand everything you were going to say. In addition to artistic talent, she had executive ability. Also enthusiasm and physical stamina."

Julia Morgan herself said, "my buildings will be my legacy... they will speak for me long after I'm gone."

Selected Buildings by Julia Morgan

Schools, Churches, Hospitals

BERKELEY
Berkeley Baptist Divinity School
  Dwight Way & Hillegas St.   1818-19
Berkeley Day Nursery auditorium
  6th St.   1927
Calvary Presbyterian Church
  Milvia St. & Virginia St.   1918-19
Saint John's Presbyterian Church
  College Ave. & Derby St.   1908-10
Thousand Oaks Baptist Church
  1821 Catalina St.   1924
University of California, Berkeley
  Hearst Mining Building   1901-07
  Greek Theater   1903
  Girton Hall   1911
  Phoebe Hearst Gymnasium   1925-26

LOS ANGELES
Marion Davies Pediatric Clinic
  11672 Louisiana Ave.   1930

OAKLAND
Chapel of the Chimes
  4499 Piedmont Ave.   1926-30
First Swedish Baptist Church
  3rd Ave. & E. 15th St.   1923-24
High Street Presbyterian Church
  Courtland St. & High St.   1919-21
Kings Daughters Home
  39th St. & Broadway   1908-12
Mills College, Oakland
  Bell Tower   1903-04
  Margaret Carnegie Library   1905-06
  Gymnasium   1909
  Ethel Moore Center   1916
  Ming Quong Girls School   1924-25
United Presbyterian Church
  College Ave.   1916-18

SAN ANSELMO
San Francisco Presbyterian
  Theological Seminary
  118 Bolinas Ave.   1921

SAN FRANCISCO
Chinese Presbyterian Mission School
  920 Sacramento St.   1908
Hamilton Methodist-Episcopal Church
  1525 Waller St.   1908
Katherine Delmar Burke School
  3025 Jackson St.   1916

Methodist Chinese Mission School
  920 Washington St.   1907-10
Ocean Avenue Presbyterian Church
  32 Ocean Ave.   1921

SANTA BARBARA
Santa Barbara County TB Sanitarium
  300 N. San Antonio Rd.   1918

SANTA CRUZ MOUNTAINS
Montezuma School for Boys
  Bear Creek Rd.   1910-11

YWCAs, Clubs, Community Centers

ASILOMAR
Pacific Grove Outside Inn   1913
Entrance gates   1913
Administration Building   1913
Chapel   1915
Guest Inn   1915
Saltwater swimming pool   1915
Visitors Lodge   1916
Hilltop Cottage   1918
Viewpoint Cottage   1918
Crocker Dining Hall   1918
Tide Inn   1923
Pinecrest   1927-28
Scripps Lodge   1927-28
Merrill Hall   1928

BERKELEY
Berkeley Women's City Club
  2315 Durant St.   1929-30
Delta Zeta sorority house
  2311 LeConte Ave.   1923
Kappa Alpha Theta sorority house
  2723 Durant St.   1908

FRESNO
Fresno YWCA offices
  Tuolumne St. & L St.   1924
Fresno YWCA residence
  1660 M St.   1922

HOLLYWOOD
Hollywood Studio Club (YWCA)
  1215 Lodi Place   1925-26

HONOLULU
University of Hawaii YWCA   1926
YWCA Metropolitan Headquarters
  1040 Richards St.   1925-26

OAKLAND
Oakland YWCA
  1515 Webster St.   1913-15
PALO ALTO
YWCA hostess house
  27 University Ave.   1916-18
PASADENA
Pasadena YWCA
  78 N. Marengo Ave.   1921
RIVERSIDE
Riverside YWCA
  3245 7th St.   1929
SALT LAKE CITY
Salt Lake City YWCA
  322 E. 3rd St. S.   1919-20
SAN DIEGO
San Diego YWCA and hostess house
  621 C St.   1917-18
SAN FRANCISCO
Chinese YWCA
  965 Clay St.   1930
Emanu-el Sisterhood Residence
  Page St. & Laguna St.   1921-22
Japanese YWCA
  1830 Sutter St.   1930
Ladies Protection & Relief Society
  3400 Laguna St.   1924-25
Native Daughters of the Golden West
  500 Baker St.   1928
Potrero Hill House Community Center
  953 De Haro St.   1921
The Residence (YWCA)
  940 Powell St.   1929-30
SAN LUIS OBISPO
San Luis Obispo Women's Club
  1800 Monterey St.   1933-34
SAN PEDRO
YWCA hostess house
  1012 C St.   1916-18
SANTA BARBARA
Santa Barbara Recreation Building
  100 E. Carillo St.   1914
SANTA MARIA
Santa Maria Women's Club
  Lincoln St. & Boone St.   1927
SARATOGA
Saratoga Foothill Women's Club
  Park Place   1915
SAUSALITO
Sausalito Women's Club
  120 Central Ave.   1916-18

Commercial Properties

BERKELEY
Edmonds apartment building
  2612-16 Regent St.   1904
Turner stores, offices, & restaurant
  2546 Bancroft Way   1938-41
LOS ANGELES
Examiner Building
  1111 S. Broadway   1915
OAKLAND
Turner shopping center & apartments
  Piedmont Ave. & 40th St.   1916
SAN FRANCISCO
Cox apartment building
  1720 Pacific Ave.   1910-11
Fairmont Hotel (reconstruction)
  California St. & Mason St. 1906-07
Hearst Building
  3rd St. & Market St.   1930s
Merchants Exchange Building
  Trading Room (interior)
  465 California St.   1906-07
Newhall apartment building
  2950 Pacific Ave.   1915-16
San Francisco Examiner Building
  5th St. & Market St.   1925
Suppo apartments, shop, & workroom
  2423-25 Polk St.   1925

Hearst Family Residences

JOLON
Hacienda
  Milpitas Ranch   1932-36
SAN SIMEON
Cottage A (Casa del Mar)   1920-22
Cottage B (Casa del Monte)   1920-22
Cottage C (Casa del Sol)   1920-22
Main building (Casa Grande) 1922-39
Neptune Pool   1924
Zoo & animal shelters   1924-35
Roman pool & tennis courts   1927-29
Poultry farm   1928-29
San Simeon village warehouses 1926-27
San Simeon village houses   1927-29
WYNTOON
Superintendent's quarters   1924
The Chalet   1925
Bear, Cinderella, & Fairy
  houses   1932-33
Bridge House   1933
Pool & pool houses   1934-35
River House   1935
Tea House   1935

Private Residences

ALAMEDA

1205 Bay St.	1912
1232 Bay St.	1909
1901 Central Ave.	1909-10
1315 Dayton Ave.	1909-10
1025 Sherman St.	1913
1121 Sherman St.	1912
1326 Sherman St.	1911

BERKELEY

1320 Arch St.	1913-14
1324 Arch St.	1910
1425 Arch St.	1910-11
862 Arlington St.	1912-13
883 Arlington St.	1905-09
2924 Ashby Ave.	1910-11
2733 Ashby Place	1908
2833 Bancroft Way	1913
1732 Berkeley Way	1908
2725 Channing Way	1908-09
2728 Channing Way	1911-12
2901 Channing Way	1905
2908 Channing Way	1907
2808 Claremont Blvd.	1914
2821 Claremont Blvd.	1928
2261 Derby St.	1909-10
2740 Derby St.	1907
2742 Derby St.	1907
2836 Derby St.	1907
2900 Derby St.	1904
2514 Etna St.	1908
2525 Etna St.	1906
2616 Etna St.	1905
2618 Etna St.	1906
1 Eucalyptus St.	1920
33 Eucalyptus St.	1921
1411 Hawthorne St.	1926
1404 Hawthorne Terr.	1911
1411 Hawthorne Terr.	1909
2317 LeConte Ave.	1908
2633 LeConte Ave.	1908-09
1841 Marin Ave.	1913
2118 Marin Ave.	1914
11 Mosswood Rd.	1929
2232 Piedmont Ave.	1909
2255 Piedmont Ave.	1904
2336 Piedmont Ave.	1913-15
2905 Piedmont Ave.	1911
2723 Regent St.	1905
2731 Regent St.	1911
1220 Spruce St.	1910-11
1626 Spruce St.	1909-10
1937 Thousand Oaks	1915
160 The Uplands	1916
2307-17 Warring St.	1911
2434 Warring St.	1911-12
2516 Warring St.	1904
2608 Warring St.	1914

CARMEL

2981 Franciscan Way	1940

CHICO

341 W. Mansion Ave.	1921

COLUSA

840 Clay St.	1918-19

DAVIS

215 Rice Lane	1914

FRESNO

733 E. Peralta Way	1912-15

LOS ALTOS

13625 Hillway St.	1913

MARYSVILLE

527 6th St.	1918
326 D St.	1919
707 F St.	1916
725 F St.	1920

OAKLAND

2020 10th Ave.	1911-12
1524 29th Ave.	1911
1284 Ashmont Ave.	1925
1031 Belle Vista Ave.	1906
385 Bellevue Ave.	1922
5440 Carlton St.	1919
360 Euclid Ave.	1908
421 Fairmont St.	1912
2626 Harrison St.	1911
9 Hillcrest Court	1916
636 Hillgirt Circle	1915-17
401 Lee St.	1907-08
769 Longridge Rd.	1918-19
686 Mariposa Ave.	1908
830 McKinley St.	1906
2065 Oakland Ave.	1911-13
339 Palm St.	1913
3001 Park Blvd.	1905
120 Richmond Blvd.	1907

PALO ALTO

423 Chaucer St.	1921-22

PEBBLE BEACH

Ronda Rd. & Cortez Rd.	1923

PETALUMA

2 Brown Court	1909
617 C St.	1909-10
707 D St.	1910-11
14 Martha St.	1929
210 West St.	1935

PIEDMONT

1 Crocker Ave.	1920-21
200 Crocker Ave.	1926
62 Farragut St.	1915
216 Hampton Rd.	1938-39
27 Highland Ave.	1909-10
111 Mountain Ave.	1912
612 Mountain Ave.	1907
246 Sea View St.	1913-14
11 Sierra Ave.	1911
45 Sierra Ave.	1913-15
49 Sierra Ave.	1913-15

SACRAMENTO

3731 T St.	1916

SAN FRANCISCO

4455 Anza St.	1926-27
3531 Clay St.	1908-09
1050 Jackson St.	1907
1052 Jackson St.	1907
3630 Jackson St.	1916-17
2511 Octavia St.	1908-09
308 Parnassus Ave.	1909-10
1010 Powell St.	1908-09
36 Presidio Terr.	1911
2820 Vallejo St.	1907

2868 Vallejo St.	1909-10
34 West Clay Park	1914
75 Yerba Buena	1927

SAN LUIS OBISPO

Zegar playhouse, Mill St.	1925

SAN MATEO

518 N. Hurlingham Ave.	1912

SAN RAFAEL

47 Fairway Drive	1909

SANTA BARBARA

430 Hot Springs Rd.	1915-16

SANTA MARIA

730 S. Broadway	1927

SAUSALITO

162 Buckley St.	1910
87 Central Ave.	1919-20

VALLEJO

728 Capital St.	1908-09

WALNUT CREEK

35 Pine Crest St.	1935

YUBA CITY

364 2nd St.	1920

For Further Reading

Boutelle, Sara Holmes. *Julia Morgan, Architect*. New York: Abbeville Press, 1988.

Isaacson, Phillip M. *Round Buildings, Square Buildings, and Buildings that Wiggle Like a Fish*. New York: Alfred A. Knopf, 1988.

Macaulay, David. *Castle*. Boston: Houghton Mifflin, 1977.

Macaulay, David. *Cathedral: The Story of Its Construction*. Boston: Houghton Mifflin, 1973.

Pelta, Kathy. *Bridging the Golden Gate*. Minneapolis: Lerner Publications, 1987.

Stern, Robert. *Pride of Place: Building the American Dream*. Boston: Houghton Mifflin, 1986.

Taylor, John. *Commonsense Architecture*. New York: William Norton, 1983.

Wilcox, Charlotte. *A Skyscraper Story*. Minneapolis: Carolrhoda Books, 1990.

Index

(Numbers in **bold face** refer to illustrations)

Acknowledgements

The illustrations have been reproduced through the courtesy of:
pp. 1, 2, 6, 10, 13, 14, 16, 18, 21, 23, 26, 29, 33, 34-35, 36, 41, 45, 47, 50, 51, 53, 54, 56-57, 63, 74-75, 79, 82, 83 (top), 88, 94, 97, 98, 99, 102, 105, 106, 107, 110, 112, 113, 114, 117, 121, Special Collections, California Polytechnic State University; p. 30, University Archives, Bancroft Library; p. 38, Library of Congress; pp. 48, 60, 65, 72, 77, 81, 85, 92, 96 (bottom), Robert Latson; pp. 59, 66, 67, 68, 69, 70, 108, National Board YWCA Archives; p. 76, British Tourist Authority; pp. 80, 84, 89, 93, Hearst Monument/John Blades; pp. 83 (bottom), 86, 91, Hearst Monument/Ken Raveill; pp. 90, 95, 100, Marc Wanamaker, Bison Archives; p. 96 (top), Hearst Monument/Ellis Sawyer; p. 102, Hearst Monument Archives/Wahlberg Collection. Cover photographs courtesy of Robert Latson.

The quoted passages have been reprinted by permission of:
pp. 7, 8, 9, 19, 21, 42, 43, 44, 52, 53, 58, 61, 62, 64, 71, 73, 81, 82, 101, 103, 104, 113, 117, 118, 119, 120, 121, *Julia Morgan History Project*, Regional Oral History Office.
pp. 7, 9, 43, 70, 121, "Designed by Julia Morgan," Harriet Rochlin. *Westways Women*, March 1976.
pp. 7, 37, 43, 89, 109, 120, "A Tycoon's Home Was His Petite Architect's Castle," Lynne Olson. *Smithsonian*, December 1985.
pp. 7, 52, 75, 76, 78, 80, *Hearst Castle*. Taylor Coffman. Santa Barbara: Sequoia Communications, 1985.
pp. 11, 21, 23, 24, 25, 27, 40, 78, 85, 88, 89, 98, 101, 103, 104, 107, 109, 110, 111, 113, 116, 117, Special Collections, California Polytechnic State University.
pp. 24, 33, 42, 47, 69, 115, *Julia Morgan, Architect*. Sara Holmes Boutelle. New York: Abbeville Press, 1988.
pp. 71, 79, *William Randolph Hearst*. Nancy Loe. Santa Barbara: Sequoia Communications, 1988.
pp. 74, 89, *It Remains to Be Seen*. Elinor Richey. Berkeley: Howell-North Books, 1973.